Power through Discourse

Edited by
Leah Kedar
Democratic National Committee
Washington, D.C.
University of Maryland
College Park, MD

 Ablex Publishing Corporation
Norwood, N.J. 07648

Library of Congress Cataloging-in-Publication Data

Power through discourse.

"Papers. . . with the exception of one subsequently invited philosophical piece, were presented in the Symposium on Language and Power at the American Anthropological Association meetings of 1982"—Introd.
Bibliography: p.
Includes index.
Contents: Discourse and power / Deborah Tannen—Language in political anthropology / Jack McIver Weatherford—The powers of language : a philosophical analysis / S. Jack Odell—[etc.]
1. Languages—Political aspects—Congresses.

2. Power (Social sciences)—Congresses. 3. Sociolinguistics—Congresses. I. Kedar, Leah. II. Symposium on Language and Power (1982 : Washington, D.C.) III. American Anthropological Association. Meeting (81st : 1982 : Washington, D.C.)
P119.3.P69 1987   306'.4   86-32029
ISBN 0-89391-328-6

Ablex Publishing Corporation
355 Chestnut Street
Norwood, New Jersey 07648

Table of Contents

*This book is dedicated to the memory of
Erving Goffman—our teacher*

General Introduction

Leah Kedar

The focus of this volume is on the relationship between *discourse* and *power*. It represents an interdisciplinary approach to the study of language and behavior in both formal, public negotiation, and in less formal, communicative interaction settings. Our central theme is that language-use plays a critical role in the attainment and/or the exercise of power. The notion of power, in the present context, is seen simply as the measure of one's ability or inability to obtain or maintain objectives, such as getting a job, winning a court case, getting elected to office, and so on, through discourse.

Clearly, the ability to achieve and maintain power is not solely an outcome of language use. Nonlinguistic social factors such as network systems, physical coercion, the ability to gather and use information effectively, and so on, all figure in political and negotiative success. As observers of communicative interaction, we are especially aware of the way in which participants use language in a manner which both reflects and critically affects the ways in which others perceive, judge, and stereotype them (Gumperz, 1982). Thus the focus of this volume is on the interaction between individual discourse strategies and the exercise of power.

A fruitful place to observe the relationship between discourse and power in social interaction is in the context of "public negotiations" (Gumperz, 1976). These are situations in which "interaction" is seen as "instrumental and goal directed." In such interactions, people are involved in win/lose situations where language-use is a critical correlate of success or failure in goal achievement. In public negotiation settings such as a job interview, a court case, or a political speech, the power of individuals to effect outcomes —through discourse—is crucial. For our purpose, then, public negotiations provide a useful locus of study through which an individual's discourse style can be examined relative to his or her successful access to power.

Public negotiations also represent communicative interactions. The study of these negotiations help us to see more clearly how language functions to facilitate interaction creatively while being bound simultaneously by cultural rules and norms of the social system in which it takes place. Thus, public negotiations display the interplay between the individual's discourse style and sociocultural constraints which affect communicative interaction. This dual character of language interaction (see Gumperz & Tannen, 1979)—i.e., that between individual discourse style, on the one hand, and social constraint on the other—is reflected in two major currents in contemporary anthropological approaches to the study of language and power. One approach emphasizes the social and political constraints which affect the process and outcome of communicative situations. This perspective, represented by a collection of papers edited by Maurice Bloch (1975) focuses on the ways in which political language is shaped by the social situation in which it takes place. Bloch expresses the relative importance attributed by this perspective to individual action versus social constraint succinctly: "Oratorical power cannot be attributed to the speaker (1975)".

An alternative approach to the study of language and power is exemplified by the collection of papers edited recently by Robert Paine (1981). In it the authors focus on the individual's ability to create the "mood" of an interaction. Paine locates the focus of this approach at the level of the relationship between individuals as social actors, each of whom "strives to have his audience see the world through his interpretation of it in his speeches." Paine views rhetoric less in terms of the cultural and sociopolitical structures affecting communicative interaction than from the perspective of the individual for whom discourse (rhetoric) is the means, if successful, of negotiating meaning with others.

The works edited by Bloch and Paine, respectively, thus reflect two different approaches to the study of language and power; each study has tended to follow a separate path of development, each has focused on a different dimension of conversational interaction. Bloch's work emphasizes the role of social structure in traditional societies as a determinant of style in political rhetoric; Paine's work emphasizes the role of the individual as social actor and his or her manipulation of elements of language style during political interaction. Anthropological studies of language and power have tended, thus far, to follow one or the other of these approaches focusing either on aspects of individual discourse style and communicative strategies, or on the sociocultural factors constraining and affecting discourse.

This volume attempts to bridge both views.

In order to achieve a fuller understanding of the ways in which discourse both actively facilitates communicative interaction and is bound by the circumstances surrounding it, we look at the way in which individual discourse style and sociocultural constraints on discourse affect and depend upon each other. We adapt an integrative approach to the study of communicative interaction combining elements of the perspectives exemplified by both Bloch and Paine.

The study of the social context of language and power should consider
ιot only such factors as age, sex, and role differentiation in relationship to
liscourse style, but also constraints imposed by institutional parameters of
liscourse associated with kinship, jural and domestic politics, and the like.
Cultural factors such as ethnicity, value systems, and ideology must also be
onsidered. In pluralistic societies, such as the United States, people of differ-
nt linguistic and ethnic backgrounds interact regularly in public negotiation
ettings. Through the study of these situations we may come to understand
nore clearly the interaction between social constraints and individual dis-
ourse style. This volume provides a venue for exploring issues related to
anguage and power in a variety of public negotiation settings. We approach
he subject from a variety of analytical perspectives, all of which taken to-
,ether contribute toward an interdisciplinary approach to the integrative
tudy of power through discourse.

The papers in this volume, with the exception of one subsequently invited
philosophical piece, were presented in the Symposium on Language and
'ower at the American Anthropological Association Meetings of 1982 in
Washington, D.C. The papers represent diverse analytical perspectives
Irawn from the disciplines of linguistics, anthropology, and philosophy,
ιnd address a range of empirical and methodological issues. Though the
nterpretative perspectives vary, our subject remains—the study of power
hrough discourse.

The book consists of several review/background papers followed by case
tudies. Tannen and Weatherford presented overview papers as commen-
aries at the Symposium. Odell was later invited to contribute a paper on
philosophical issues bearing on the analysis of language and power. The
hree case study sections are distinguished both by the type of social interac-
ion examined (e.g., formal jural settings vs. informal everyday settings) as
vell as by the level of analysis of discourse involved. Shuy and Walker focus
heir analyses at the level of discourse elements while Philips and Agar look
o the social contexts of discourse. Varenne, McDermott and Tylbor treat
neta-discourse issues.

Tannen provides an integrative commentary on themes in the case studies
ocusing upon their respective representations of power as a *linguistic* con-
:eption. She also draws our attention to the crucial role of ambiguity in
ower-consequential communicative interaction settings, and cautions us
:oncerning the potential for use and abuse of our own knowledge about language, power, and manipulation.

Weatherford traces some important historical dimensions of the background of anthropological approaches to the study of power and language
.n Great Britain and in the United States. He sets the case studies in the con-
:ext of these two traditions and focuses on their respective representations

of power as an anthropological conception. Weatherford sees the contributions in this volume as marking a new course in linguistic and anthropological research which builds upon both earlier traditions in the study of language and power.

Odell presents a philosophical background discussion of elements of the analysis of language and power which figure implicitly and explicitly in all of the subsequent case studies. Like Weatherford, who speaks to the anthropological assumptions underlying contemporary studies of language and power, Odell draws our attention to the rich tradition of twentieth century philosophy of language which underpins virtually all of our current discussion on meaning, sense, ambiguity, and understanding. These philosophical issues are prominent aspects of any discussion of meaning and social context and they inform the assumptions, methods, and interpretations of language and power found throughout this volume.

Shuy and Walker look at aspects of language use and abuse in dramatically power-imbalanced interaction settings. Theirs are studies of the deliberate coercive manipulation of others by powerful adversaries who maintain information monopolies and rigid control of interaction. Utilizing discourse analysis methodologies, Shuy and Walker explore dimensions of the systematic exploitation of ambiguity, and the pervasive deceptive language-use strategies of adversarial circumstances.

Philips and Agar apply ethnographic methods to the study of the social dimensions of language interaction in status differentiated settings. They point to the social structural constraints upon language interaction in power-imbalanced public negotiation settings.

Varenne as well as McDermott and Tylbor shift our attention to the less formal domains of language and power found in the home and classroom, respectively. Unlike Shuy and Walker, who try to explain how people systematically deceive and coerce one another through discourse, or Phillips and Agar, who show how social constraints confound communication, Varenne together with McDermott and Tylbor demonstrates how people do, in fact, manage to understand one another successfully by active collusion in spite of the inherent ambiguity of discourse itself.

REFERENCES

Bloch, M. (1975). *Political language and oratory in traditional society.* New York: Academic Press.

Gumperz, J.J. (1976). Language, communication and public negotiations. In R. Sanday (Ed.), *Anthropology and the public interest: Fieldwork and theory.* New York: Academic Press.

Gumperz, J.J. (1982). *Discourse strategies.* New York: Cambridge University Press.

Gumperz, J.J., & Tannen, D. (1979). Individual and social differences in language use (pp. 305–324). In C.J. Fillmore, D. Kempler, & W. Wang (Eds.), *Individual differences in language ability and language behavior.* New York: Academic Press.

Paine, R. (1981). *Politically speaking.* Philadelphia: Institute for the Study of Human Issues.

Part I

PERSPECTIVES ON LANGUAGE
AND POWER

Chapter 1

Remarks on Discourse and Power

Deborah Tannen

Georgetown University

Following is a transcription, with only minor revisions of remarks that were made in the role of respondent to the papers delivered at the session, "Power Through Discourse." I begin these remarks with two general and unrelated observations about the papers gathered here, and then move to a discussion of the question suggested by them: What is power? Then I comment on three linguistic phenomena that are discussed in many of these papers: questions, topic, and interruptions. Based on these observations, I caution against too hasty correlations of discourse phenomena with underlying forces such as power, showing how the same phenomenon can be evidence of different, even opposite, motivations, depending on the context and roles of participants. I illustrate this with the linguistic concept of power and solidarity. Finally, I end with a caution about the power of our own expertise as analysts of interaction.

The papers collected here can be seen in descending order of focus on power: they discuss increasingly less concrete manifestations of power, but no less embodiment of power. Reordered in this way, the three papers based on the legal setting (those by Philips, Walker, and Shuy) discuss the most extreme and obvious form of power. The public negotiation situation considered by Agar is next. After that comes the McDermott and Tylbor study of school interaction, and finally Varenne's analysis of the subtle power distinctions in family talk. It is particularly enlightening to be able to compare discourse in these diverse settings, even as it is particularly hazardous, given the differences in so many aspects of the discourse studied and the theoretical and methodological approaches taken to them.

An important aspect of the papers concerned with the legal setting which was not their focus is, as Philips puts it, that some of the participants are in the know and some are not. This in itself gives those in the know a kind of power, at the same time that their power gives them access to knowledge. One aspect of their knowledge is their awareness that the talk created on the spot in face-to-face interaction was really not the significant end product. Rather, the encounters yielded a permanent record which would look different in many ways from the oral event, and which might be more important in the long run.

This is an interesting and important factor. The nature of truth and reality that we expect in face-to-face conversation is different from what we expect in writing. As suggested by McDermott and Tylbor, we really don't expect —and even less ever get—an explicit kind of truth in conversation, as we expect in writing.

Consider, in this regard, the discourse produced by three of the participants in the legal setting. In Shuy's data, a government agent knew that the interaction in which he was participating was being taped. It is likely, then, that he was asking questions with an eye to what the video record would look like. In the case of the deposition (Walker), the lawyer was aware that the proceeding would yield a transcript, had seen innumerable such transcripts in the past, and had seen their effects on the outcomes of cases. The deposed witness had probably never experienced or seen any and would therefore draw upon her experience in interaction as a reference point in deciding how to talk. In the case of the change of plea proceeding (Philips), the judge is familiar with court transcripts and their status as legal documents; the defendant is not.

Such a distinction between those aware of the resultant written record and those focused only on the current interaction is common in interaction in institutional settings. Similarly, the professionals, in numerous contexts, are doing something they do all the time, whereas the others are doing something they do rarely.[1] Thus doctors, lawyers, and teachers, in examining rooms, courts, and classrooms (respectively, of course) are doing business-as-usual on their home turf, while their clients pass through the system, often confused and always ignorant of the intricacies of the system. This suggests a problem inherent in understanding power in discourse. As McDermott puts it, "the meaning is really in the situation," and most of what people understand in interaction can't be located in the words spoken. This explains, in part, Varenne's suggestion that when we look at a transcript, what we see is very different from what went on moment to moment.

When we look at a videotape or transcript, we see both more and less than what actually occurred. There is less there because much of what people understand in interaction is not derived from the words spoken. There is more there because of the inherent indeterminacy of speech which is lost when it is written down. Written discourse appears definite where the spoken

---

[1] This may obtain in many professions. In the movie *Klute,* a call girl (played by Jane Fonda) tells her therapist that when she meets a client, he is nervous but she is not. This, she says, is just fine, presumably because it puts her in control—an interesting perspective on the question of who has the power in such an interaction.

discourse was indefinite. This can be seen even in the uttering of words. When a word is uttered it doesn't have a perfect form. Maybe it was realized in reduced form like "n" in "ham'n'eggs" or not uttered at all like "do you" in "Wanna go?" But when written, "ham and eggs," the word "and" is fully realized, and, unless the intention is to mirror speech, "wanna go?" will become "Do you want to go?" in writing. Words as spoken are typically reduced, slurred, run together, or even purposely ambiguous.[2] Their meaning is mediated by how they are spoken. When written, words are discrete, definite, and committed.

WHAT IS POWER?

With this as a basis, I want to tackle the question, *What is power?* The papers collected here (like much current conversation) bristle with words like power, manipulation, and control. What are the relationships among these? Is manipulation the same as power, or is manipulation what you do when you don't have power? Is "control" the same in "control of topic" and "control of the trucking industry"? Is power in court the same power as power in a family relationship, or as the power of production?

I suggest that the notion of power or control is always metaphoric when applied to interaction and discourse. Is there any situation in which power is equal? It is misleading, I believe, to reify power as if there is one source of it and somebody has it and someone else doesn't. I suggest that there are many different kinds of power and influence that are interrelated and have varied manifestations. When people are taking different roles, it may not be the case that one has power and one doesn't, but that they have different kinds of power, and they are exercising it in different ways.

This is similar to a caution that Frake (1977) and others have sounded about application of frames theory. They warn against assuming that frames are static and can be identified, as if one could walk into a situation and say, "Show me your frames." Similarly, we cannot confront a situation and ask, "Okay. Where's the power?" Power may be there in different forms and in different ways—all constantly changing in dynamic response to the behavior of others.

To conclude this section, I refer to a line from Varenne's paper: "A power analysis of an interaction is not, strictly speaking, an analysis of interaction." This is important to remember. When we study an interaction and ask what is going on, we are necessarily applying interpretations from other

---

[2] An instance of intended ambiguity in writing is when schoolchildren, uncertain of how to spell a word, intentionally make a mess in place of the questionable letter(s) in hopes that the teacher will assume the student intended to correct a wrong form with a right one, or will simply discern the correct form in there somewhere and move on.

coherence systems (a term from Gregory Bateson that Varenne uses). This is necessarily so because without a lot of background knowledge, interaction is incomprehensible. But it must be borne in mind so that our interpretations can be monitored and checked as we go, rather than being accepted as concrete.

DISCOURSE DEVICES

I will now comment on two discourse devices that are discussed in these chapters and have been much discussed in linguistics: questions and topic.

Questions

There has been a great deal of research on the form and function of questions in interaction. Addressing a general issue first, I would observe that there are some contradictory findings about the power of questions in various papers here and elsewhere, suggesting that their function is complex. For example, Walker tells us, and cites others who tell us, that lawyers' and judges' rights to demand an answer to their questions is a manifestation of their power. This sounds right.

At the same time, however, William Hall (in a paper that was included in the panel which gave rise to this volume but is not included here) tells us that in white as compared to black families he studied, twice as many adult-generated questions got no response from children. Would we therefore want to say that white adults have less power than their black counterparts, because they do not demand a response to their questions?

In a study of talk in a pediatric medical setting, Tannen and Wallat (1983) found that the mother "asked questions" which did not have the form of questions. She stated a concern, and the doctor responded as if she had asked a question. Now in some sense it would seem that the mother must have a tremendous amount of power in that setting because she got the doctor to answer her questions without even asking them. Such analyses have been made of indirect speech acts. It has been argued, for example, that an employer can get a butler or maid to open a window simply by stating, "It's hot in here," because of superior status or power. Yet we would not want to make that interpretation about the doctor/patient setting. On the contrary, the person in power in a medical setting is conventionally assumed to be the physician. If the physician responds to the mother's indirect questions, she does so by choice—and her exercise of choice is a reflection of her power. This choice, however, does not show up in the discourse; we find it in our real world knowledge about medical settings and possible responses to indirectness in discourse.

Ervin-Tripp (1978) wanted to find out at what age young children were able to understand indirect requests. She devised an experiment by which she showed child subjects a picture of children applying finger-paints to a wall, at the moment when their mother walked in. In one case, the mother is shown to say, "Stop painting the wall!" In another she says, "Are you painting the wall?" In yet a third, she says nothing. Ervin-Tripp expected to find that very young children would not understand that "Are you painting the wall?" is an indirect way to get them to stop. She found instead that it made no difference what the mother said. It was sufficient for her to appear for the children to understand that she was telling them to stop doing what they were doing—an activity that all children recognize as cause for adult disapproval.

While some have argued that those in power may use indirect requests (or, as in Ervin-Tripp's study, the most indirect request of all—silence), others have suggested that only a person in a position of power can make a direct request like "Shut the window." In other words, the meaning is in the context rather than the words spoken or not spoken.

In a study of indirectness in discourse among Greeks and Americans (Tannen 1981), I found (and similar observations have frequently been made for Japanese) that when Greeks say "yes" they may mean "no". This surpasses Shuy's point: Not only does "uhuh" not mean "yes," but "yes" doesn't necessarily mean "yes" either. For example, a Greek woman explained to me that when she wanted to do something she had to ask her husband (or, previously, her father) first. If he said, "Yes, you can go if you want," she understood that she shouldn't. If he said, "Yes, of course, you should go," then she understood that she could.

It would be tempting here to conclude that Greek women are so oppressed that they must obey even hinted preferences—"Your wish is my command." But bear in mind that the woman might actually not feel commanded. She may feel—and prefer to feel—that she is choosing to do what someone else wants because of her relationship to him. (For discussion of indirectness see Tannen 1981, 1986). So the situation is very complex in terms of whether or not the man in these situations is exercising more or less power by communicating indirectly. My fear is that often, in interpretation, we begin with our real-world assumptions about who has power and who doesn't, and interpret the use of various linguistic devices in support of those assumptions.

Topic

Topic is a phenomenon that has received much recent attention from linguists. The inclusion of data from family interaction is particularly enlightening here, because it is one of the more unfocused (to borrow a term from Scollon & Scollon, 1981) forms of discourse, in comparison to relatively focused and comparatively less common forms of discourse studied in the other papers, and frequently studied by linguists.

It is suggested in this volume and elsewhere that the person who controls the topic is the person who controls the interaction. This is seen in Shuy's and Walker's as well as other legal data. But in most settings, a topic cannot become a topic simply because someone raised it; someone else must pick it up. There has to be, in McDermott's terms, collusion. In this regard, it is not sufficient to consider what is in the transcript or even in the interaction. We have to ask what else could have happened, in order to see that what did occur was a joint production.

In a study of a single dinner table conversation (Tannen, 1984), I tried to count how many topics each participant had raised. I found, however, that decisions about what constituted a topic and who raised it were highly interpretive. For example, an extended discussion centered on the question of whether adopted children more closely resemble their biological or adoptive parents. An obvious conclusion was that this topic—adoption—was raised by the participant, Peter, whose comment was the first that could be considered "on" this topic. He had commented that he had read an article about a study which found that the IQ's of adopted children more closely resembled those of their biological parents.

But how accurate would it be to say that Peter raised the topic of adoption? Discussion centered on the topic of adoption only because others picked it up and channeled it in this way. If no one had picked up this topic, we would not count it as one, and yet Peter's behavior would have been the same. Furthermore, the fact that discussion centered on adoption, rather than IQ's, is the doing of other participants. Later in the dinner table conversation, discussion turns to whether intelligence is inherited or nurtured, and whether or not, in consequence, educational funds should concentrate on gifted or disadvantaged children. At that point Peter returned to the article he had read, saying that's why he found it interesting. It is likely that the adoption aspect was not the topic he intended to raise, and it is not clear that he intended to "raise a topic" as compared to "making a comment." Thus a topic becomes a topic, as a statement may become a question, because of the way others respond to it.

Continuing to focus on someone else's topic may give them power, but it may also be seen to reflect the power of the attention-giver. Varenne observes that whereas initially the wife in his study does not pick up on her husband's introduction of the china closet topic, she gets back to it and then makes an exaggerated show of interest in it by asking a whole series of questions about it. The china closet is still in some sense the husband's topic, but whether or not it was realized as one, and how much or little attention was paid to it, was the doing of the wife.

We should not, therefore, be hasty to correlate surface features with underlying forces such as power. Features used in one case by the powerful can be used in other cases by the powerless.

Another linguistic device that can be understood in this light is interruption, seen very dramatically in Shuy's data in which, as he explains, those who were taping an interaction as part of a scam were watching it from another room and were able to see when the target was about to say something that they didn't want on the record. They could then interrupt the interaction and prevent it from being said. This ability to obstruct by interrupting grows out of their being in control—in power. Yet the people who use interruption in just this way, in Varenne's study, are the ones lacking in power. For them, interruption is a last resort bid for attention. Whenever the husband and wife begin a positive interaction with each other, the children interrupt them.

CONCLUSION: VERSATILITY OF LINGUISTIC DEVICES

I would like to end with some thoughts about the potential double meaning in any message. Perhaps the most relevant way of demonstrating this is the linguistic concept of power and solidarity, which are both served by the same linguistic means. For example, I may call you by your first name because we are friends—solidarity—or because I am superior to you in status—power. Ralph Fasold (cited and discussed in Tannen, 1986) gives an example of the misinterpretation of such a sign by an old woman who said she was really in tight with the nurses in her nursing home because they called her by her first name. Fasold suspected she was mistaking their lack of respect for her advanced years as a sign of solidarity.

This suggests a very crucial question about whether the perception of an exercise of power, of control, of domination, is always synonymous with the intent to exercise it. If a doctor or professor addresses a patient or student by first name in order to be friendly—solidarity—he or she may be taken to be patronizing. This particular ambiguity could be solved by asking whether the client or student addressed by first name is entitled to reciprocate. But even if the form of address is reciprocal, it is usually the doctor or professor who has the prerogative of "allowing" the patient or student to use this form of address, and this itself is a sign of power or status. Thus people in possession of socially defined power are constrained in how their words and actions are likely to be interpreted, quite apart from their intentions, just as much as are those out of power.

A second word of caution is suggested by the title of this volume: power through discourse. I have had occasion to write about language for popular audiences and have found that publishers and agents are most interested in a book about how to achieve power through discourse. People want a how-to book in which experts help them exercise power over others.

It is clear that linguistic and interactive skill does give people power over others. But we have to think about how we as experts want to be of service to people in their pursuit of this goal. We would all agree, I think, that it would be good to help medical patients, witnesses, job applicants, and innocent targets of scams to get more control through talk. That is, we can help people protect themselves against those who have more power than they. But what if those who are planning a scam, or con artists, or advertisers, or any of a range of manipulaters, get hold of our writings and find ways to better accomplish their unseemly goals? I will end, therefore, on a note of caution, not only with respect to the manipulation of the concept of power in our theoretical paradigms and analytical frameworks, but also with respect to the uses our work may be put to, as we go beyond theory to application. In other words, we have to consider seriously our own power, when we move beyond the comfortable academic analysis of discourse to the real world exercise of power.

REFERENCES

Ervin-Tripp, S. (1978). Whatever happened to communicative competence? In B. Kachru (Ed.), *Linguistics in the seventies: Directions and prospects*. Studies in the Linguistic Sciences, Vol. 8 No. 2, pp. 238-58.

Frake, C.O. (1977). Plying frames can be dangerous: Some reflections on methodology in cognitive anthropology. *The Quarterly Newsletter of the Institute for the Study of Comparative Human Cognition, 1,* 1-7.

Scollon, R., & Scollon, B.K. (1981). Narrative, literacy and face in interethnic communication. Norwood, NJ: Ablex.

Tannen, D. (1981). Indirectness in discourse: Ethnicity as conversational style. *Discourse Processes, 4,* 221-238.

Tannen, D. (1984). Conversational style: Analyzing talk among friends. Norwood, NJ: Ablex.

Tannen, D. (1986). *That's not what I meant!: How conversational style makes or breaks your relations with others.* New York: William Morrow.

Tannen, D., & Wallat, C. (1983). Doctor/mother/child communication: Linguistic analysis of a pediatric interaction. In S. Fisher & A.D. Todd (Eds.), *The social organization of doctor-patient communication.* Washington, DC: The Center for Applied Linguistics.

Chapter 2

Language in Political Anthropology

Jack McIver Weatherford

Macalester College
St. Paul, Minnesota

The present volume marks a major step in the reintegration of language and power variables in anthropology. It seems quite odd that these two variables would have been separated in the first place. After all, the exercise of power nearly always depends upon language and speech acts far more than it does on physical force, even when such force may be the ultimate sanction behind a particular speech act. By a curious set of academic and political circumstances, however, the consideration of speech and power in anthropology went separate ways—to opposite sides of the Atlantic. Power became the centerpiece of social anthropology in Britain, while language and speech became ever more important to the various kinds of cultural anthropology disciplines developed in the United States.

In some of the earlier anthropological works, most notably those of Lewis Henry Morgan, power and discourse were given prominent emphasis in the general mixture of cultural analysis which included everything from religion to basket-weaving. To a lesser extent, this was even true of the speculative armchair works of James Frazier, Edward Tylor, and Henry Maine. In Britain, both A.R. Radcliffe-Brown and Bronislaw Malinowski pulled anthropology into a much more narrow and more social focus. Eventually, this social focus made anthropology in Britain almost anticultural as well as antihistorical in pursuit of the purely social analysis. Anthropology in America remained cultural and therefore concerned with language; however, since American anthropologists dealt exclusively with the powerless peoples in the United States, they tended to ignore power in anything other than an historical context.

THE RISE OF POLITICAL ANTHROPOLOGY

As a distinct subfield, political anthropology was a product of British anthropology and imperialism. In some regards, the study of political power

11

became nearly synonymous with the particular brand of social anthropology practiced in Britain. In this early form of applied anthropology, the discipline was playing handmaiden to the Empire. The wide expanse of the British Empire embraced many different tribes, ethnic groups, communities, and nations, all of which needed to be managed by the comparatively small population of Great Britain. The British, as it were, had enough trouble on their hands in the constant struggle to manage neighboring Ireland and in the repeated threats of war which came from mainland European nations such as Germany, Italy, and Russia.

As the twentieth century wore on and British troubles increased, the Empire needed ever more ingenious ways to maximize the exploitation of its subject peoples while minimizing the use of British subjects and force. To achieve these seemingly contradictory goals, the colonial administration needed to know as much as possible about the traditional governments and native lines of power and authority. The solution was to use the natives to exploit the natives. In pursuit of the appropriate information to accomplish this, a whole generation of anthropologists and their graduate students received funding through various parts of the colonial administration to study the tribal systems of government. A particular problem for the colonial government was how to control those peoples such as the Nuer who had no chiefs who could be bribed, no aristocracy which could be subverted or converted, no kings who could be deposed or captured, and in general no governing apparatus which could be appropriated and used by His Majesty's bureaucrats. This, then, proved to be one of the most fertile fields for anthropological investigation, and much ink was spilled in the quest to understand the acephalous society or the anarchic state, as shown in Evans-Pritchard's *The Nuer* (1940).

With this new mission, anthropology in Britain changed quickly and radically. It abandoned anything which pertained to evolution or even history; the physical artifacts of the people became as useless to the new anthropology as did physical measurements of the body. That whole hodgepodge of eccentric variables bequeathed from the time of Tylor withered to a small number of social factors very narrowly defined. The new focus became the present and how the social system worked at that one moment. Power was a major part of this new focus, but it was handled in a very abstract manner which often soared far above the everyday realities.

As the British Empire began to crumble, the sociopolitical anthropologists were adrift without a major financial backer and without a clear theoretical focus which could serve any purpose other than to fill the bureaucratic reports of the colonial offices. Casting about for a new focus and a way to continue their researches, anthropologists in Britain rediscovered some of the older concerns of symbols, myths, rituals, and even, to a limited extent, language. using a combination of variables from the older forms of anthropology, from French anthropology, and in extreme cases of need, from

American anthropology, a new generation of political anthropologists in Britain began altering the old structural-functional approach. This was very clearly shown in Edmund Leach's publication of *Political Systems of Highland Burma* in 1954.

Following Leach's work, the consideration of power in British anthropology took several directions. Leach himself became ever more interested in French structuralism rather than political anthropology. The new directions opened by Leach pointed in part to the new political work of Abner Cohen in which politics and acts of power are inseparable from the symbolic context in which they occur and are acted out. Language is once again an integral part of the process. Another line of inquiry in Leach pointed toward the action approaches of Frederick Barth and F.G. Bailey, for whom speech and power united in not just the ritual chants and symbolic forms of address, but also in the natural activities of people in everyday situations.

POWER IN AMERICAN ANTHROPOLOGY

In the United States, the study of politics and power was as slow to develop in anthropology as was the study of language and speech in British anthropology. Unlike their English colleagues, the American anthropologists lacked whole, intact native groups available for study. American anthropologists faced only small, broken, and defeated people ravaged by disease and living largely at the mercy of government bureaucrats and a few private benevolent organizations and churches. Anthropologists in the United States saw little more than the "shreds and patches" of once independent and vigorous social groups. Power was exercised over these people but not through them. Everyone from the bureaucrats in Washington to the anthropologists in the universities seemed to agree that the Indian tribes were dying entities which could not be saved, much less utilized by American society the same way that the British could utilize their subject populations.

In such a context, the focus of anthropology in the United States became the salvaging of as much information as possible about all of the native groups, their language, their history, rituals, arts, and in brief, anything which was still available for collection and analysis. American anthropology, then, focused on history and culture rather than behavior and social interaction. Lacking large-scale kinship organizations, for example, American anthropologists studied kinship terminology and classification rather than the fission and fusion of lineage systems. The actual social units, such as clans, moieties, and warrior societies, had mostly been ripped apart by war, forced relocation, epidemics, alcohol, and the other shocks of conquest. But the language was still there; in many cases, it was almost the only part of a culture left intact by the time the anthropologist arrived.

Rather than studying the everyday uses of power, anthropologists became interested in the abstract principles of native law or with histories of how things had been organized and how disputes had been handled. The research of E. Adamson Hoebel (1940; 1960), for example detailed the legal systems of the Comanche and the Cheyenne in a way which was much different from the British anthropologists of the same time who were able to work with still intact African groups. Another branch of American research was devoted to classifying political systems and seeking their origins. This stretches from Robert Lowie's *The Origin of the State* in 1927 to Ronald Cohen and Elman R. Service's editing of *Origins of the State: The Anthropology of Political Evolution* in 1978. All of this, however, was as far from the study of power in everyday life as the study of kinship terminology and classification systems was from the study of family interaction.

A new emphasis on power, language, and human interaction in American anthropology began to emerge with the 1966 publication of *Political Anthropology,* edited by Marc Swartz, Victor Turner, and Arthur Tuden. Two years later, in *Local Level Politics,* Swartz stressed an interactional analysis of political action and language in terms which were as applicable to the Bena of Tanzania as to the politicans of Washington. This new emphasis on the process of political events focused on speech in the forms of oratory, metaphor, persuasion, and explanation.

POWER AND LANGUAGE

The renewed emphasis on language and power as two different aspects of the same phenomenon occurred on both sides of the Atlantic at about the same time but in different ways. In 1975, Maurice Bloch edited a set of papers which was published as *Political Language and Oratory in Traditional Society.* At almost the same time, an American collection came out edited by William and Jean O'Barr under the simpler title of *Language and Politics* (1976).

Bloch's analysis and the papers he selected stressed formal language as used in political contexts which were often highly ritualized. Bloch was particularly concerned with the way such language acted as a determining influence on the outcome of these political events. Formal speech rules and the norms of politeness, once set in motion in a particular interaction, were often more important than the actors themselves. The rules had a binding effect which made the final resolution inevitable. This was effected through a number of hidden controls operating in the conventions and procedures of discourse. This removed the exercise of power beyond the actions of any single individual in a particular case.

The papers edited by O'Barr exhibit far greater concern with language as a political resource available for use by different actors as well as a political constraint on all the actors. Depending on the situation and the ingenuity of the participants, language and the rules of discourse and rhetoric could be manipulated in various ways. Thus language could be used by one actor to try to limit the possible behaviors and responses of another actor, but the success would depend more on the talents of the individual than the rules of the language.

The present volume advances and builds upon the analyses in both the Bloch and O'Barr volumes in looking at speech as both a shaping variable of human interaction and as a resource for use by individual actors. In Roger Shuy's analysis of the covert FBI tape recordings of Senator Harrison Williams, we see in exact detail how language and the rules of politeness can shape and push along interactions in ways which the participants may have little choice but to accept. The rules of speech and politeness compel agreements where there may, in fact, be no agreement. Thus the person who establishes the initial agenda and context of an interaction exercises tremendous power beyond what would be apparent on the surface of events.

Anne Graffam Walker (see Chapter 5) takes the focus of study to the deposition process in which lawyers question witnesses. In breaking down the types of questions into nine varieties based on the kinds of responses the lawyer wants, Walker shows how the skillful use of questions by the lawyer can shape the responses of the witness and grant the witness varying amounts of verbal freedom. Thus, the ability of the individual actors in using language rules to their own advantage is more important than the precise rule.

In moving further into the more formalized aspects of court proceedings, Susan Urmston Philips (see Chapter 6) introduces the variable of respective social status of the participants in shaping each other's verbal behavior. She shows that the amount of constraint is not the same for all participants. The higher the social status of the actor, the greater freedom he or she has to respond to the speech of a lower status individual. The relative status of the individuals is, of course, a factor already set prior to the interaction and, at least in the case of courtroom sessions, is not negotiable.

Michael Agar's (Chapter 7) article changes the pace and context of the analysis from the legal system to the regulatory process of the Federal government. In examining the hearings of the Interstate Commerce Commission, Agar picks out the major themes of discourse and, in this particular instance, shows how such thematic analysis can point out the failure of communication. The message which the small carriers wanted to convey to the commission was simply not getting across, even though the commission was sympathetic and wanted to help the small carriers.

These analyses of language and power in the formal contexts of court or regulatory commission are complemented by the less formal interactions studied by John Dore and R.P. Mcdermott (see Chapter 9) in the school and Hervé Varenne's (see Chapter 8) work in the home. Both of these works illustrate the difficulties and the importance of doing naturalistic observations outside of formal contexts.

Varenne's analysis shows that speech acts are shaped not just by the immediate situation, context, or interaction, but by very basic parts of the social relations of the actors as well. Marital strain, tension, or conflict can be present in even the most innocuous of interactions, not necessarily as a part of the discussion at hand but as background information. Such information can be extracted in much the same way that a speaker's accent can be extracted from or ignored during any kind of interaction regardless of the content of the discussion. For Varenne, speech becomes saturated with the social relations of the participants. In seeking to link up speech acts of small interactional sequences with the larger social picture, Varenne is helping to bridge the gap between the microlevel to which much of linguistic analysis so closely adheres and the macrolevel at which so much of political analysis soars. For language and power to be considered together, it is necessary that they be analyzed at the same level of abstraction. The present volume as a whole makes considerable progress toward bringing them together.

THE ETHNOGRAPHY OF AMERICA

In addition to carrying on the work already begun in the area of language and power, the present volume blazes a long-needed path toward an ethnography of power in America. Over the past few decades, anthropologists of all types have moved toward building a more representative ethnography of life in the United States. Yet, of all the subdisciplines of anthropology, political anthropology has had the least to contribute. British anthropologists have not been as remiss, as evidenced in Abner Cohen's study of Anglo-Jewish families and the City Men of London (1974). F.G. Bailey has studied university politics on both sides of the Atlantic (1977) and has used national politics in the United States as well as those of his native England and of India. Still, this is a long way from an ethnography of power in America.

This set of papers makes a decisive and much-needed move toward building a much broader ethnographic base. In doing so, these researchers point the way for future research in these areas. We need more analyses of a diversity of law-enforcement agencies as well as the FBI. We need more exhaustive studies of the higher courts as well as of lower court proceedings, and we need to know more about the interactions of lawyers, judges, and defendants or witnesses in informal settings outside of the courtroom. We need studies of the jury process and of meetings in the judge's chambers. Anthropologists should enter all kinds of government regulatory offices, as well as agencies in the executive and legislative branches. At the same time, we need to expand the notion of power outside of government offices and into the offices of corporations which manage the finances and the flow of communications in the United States. In its traditional emphasis on informal organizations as well as formal ones, anthropology has a unique perspective and methodology lacking in the other academic disciplines concerned with power.

While building this empirical body of knowledge about power in modern American society, anthropology with its tradition of holistic studies is also in a position to show how all of this is integrated within the greater fabric of American life and culture. The political themes of truckers testifying before the Interstate Commerce Commission and the themes of conflict within the home of an American family or within a criminal court are all part of the same culture. It is the discovery of the patterns underlying all of them as well as other areas of power that anthropology has as its task.

It is also in the application of anthropological knowledge and insights that political anthropologists have been remiss. While anthropologists who specialize in diverse areas from nutrition or aging to ethnicity or economics have managed to take an active role in applying anthropological knowledge to the power process in this country, political anthropologists have been silent. The present volume, however, shows that it is possible for anthropologists to work on issues of theoretical interest in the study of power and expand the consideration to items of practical interest and application. What is particularly significant is that the application aspects of these studies are available to nonanthropologists from a variety of professions. These include lawyers and government officials as well as teachers and family counselors.

It is probably inevitable that in becoming active in researching issues of importance to various parties in political or legal struggles, some anthropologists will become involved in the struggles themselves. The research and the researcher may be pulled in as resources by one side or another in a legal or political struggle. Even this, however, can be instructive and should be analyzed as one half of the participant-observation method of our science. Partisan politics are not necessarily inimical to the accumulation of knowledge. The work of Max Weber (1947), for example, benefited greatly from his participation as a member of the German team negotiating the Versailles Treaty after the First World War. Even though his task of helping protect the interests of Germany may not have been popular with many academics of the era, he was able to transcend the immediate problem of Germany versus the Allies to say a great deal about power in society. It may have been his practical political work in combination with his academic studies that made him so sensitive to the whole problem of objectivity in the social sciences. As anthropologists become more active in different arenas in their own societies, the scope of knowledge can not help but expand.

In conclusion, the works in this volume help to expand the scope of power analysis in the modern world; yet, at the same time, this volume stands as a continuation of both the American and British traditions of political analysis. Of just as much importance, however, the present works push ahead the ethnography of power and politics in the United States.

REFERENCES

Bailey, F.G. (1970). *Strategems and spoils.* Oxford: Basil Blackwell.
Bailey, F.G. (1977). *Morality and expediency.* Oxford: Basil Blackwell.
Bailey, F.G. (1983). *The tactical use of passion.* Ithaca, NY: Cornell University Press.
Barth, F. (1959). *Political leadership among the swat Pathans.* London: Athalone.
Bloch, M. (Ed.). (1975). *Political language and oratory in traditional society.* New York: Academic Press.
Cohen, A. (1974). *Two-dimensional man.* London: Routledge & Kegal Paul.
Cohen, R., & Service, E.R. (Eds.). (1978). *Origins of the state.* Philadelphia: Institute for the Study of Human Issues.
Evans-Pritchard, E.E. (1940). *The Nuer.* Oxford: Oxford University Press.
Hoebel, E.A. (1940). *The political organization and law ways of the Comanche Indians.* Washington, DC: AAA Memoir 54.
Hoebel, E. (1960). *The Cheyenne.* New York: Holt, Rinehart & Winston.
Leach, E.R. (1954). *Political systems of Highland Burma.* Boston: Beacon Press.
Leach, E. (1961). *Rethinking anthropology.* London: Athalone.
Lewellen, T.C. (1983). *Political anthropology.* South Hadley, MA: Bergin & Garvey.
Lowie, R.H. (1962). *The origin of the state.* New York: Russell & Russell (originally published 1927).
Maine, H. (1861). *Ancient law.* London: J. Murray.
Morgan, L.H. (1851). *League of the Iroquois.* Rochester, NY: Sage & Brothers.
O'Barr, W.M., & O'Barr, J.F. (1976). *Language and politics.* The Hague: Mouton.
Service, E.R. (1962). *Primitive social organizations* (2nd ed.), New York: Random House.
Service, E. (1975). *Origins of the state and civilization.* New York: W.W. Norton.
Swartz, M. (1968). *Local-level politics.* Chicago: Aldine.
Swartz, M., & Jordan, D.K. (1976). *Anthropology: Perspective on humanity.* New York: John Wiley & Sons.
Swartz, M., Turner, V., & Tuden, A. (1966). *Political anthropology.* Chicago: Aldine.
Weber, M. (1947). *Theory of social and economic organization* (T. Parsons, ed.). London: William Hodge.

Chapter 3

The Powers of Language: A Philosophical Analysis

S. Jack Odell
University of Maryland

INTRODUCTION

To ask how one group or individual uses language to control or manipulate another group or individual is to focus upon the negative aspects of communication. The word 'manipulative' is a term of negative appraisal. *Linguistic maneuvering,* however, to coin an expression which is neutral in valuative connotation, need not be, and, in fact, frequently is not manipulative. Discourse is often informative, productive, revealing, beneficial, provocative, entertaining, enjoyable, and altogether rewarding. Language has many powers or functions. It can be used to warn, inform, teach, discuss, praise, honor, promise, and record history, as well as to mislead, harm, deceive, betray, control, or manipulate. In what follows I will attempt to provide an account of those parameters of language which *any* discussion of linguistic effectiveness must recognize. My analysis aims to be universally applicable, not restricted to the negative aspects of discourse. It will delineate the dimensions of effectiveness ingrained in the fibers of natural languages like French, German, Italian, Greek, Chinese, Russian, English, and so on. I will provide a general account of linguistic maneuvering, which will include, among other things, an account of the basic dimensions and fundamental elements of communication, with emphasis upon what it means to talk about meaning or sense. I will explicate H.P. Grice's (1969) distinction between what a sentence means (*sentential meaning*) and what it might mean on some particular occasion (*contextual meaning*). In the case of sentential meaning my explication provides an analysis of: (1) when a linguistic ex-

This paper was written while the author was on sabbatical leave from the University of Maryland. I wish to thank the University of Maryland for their support.

pression in a given sentence is used in a *different* sense than it is in another sentence (multivocality); (2) when a linguistic expression means the *same* thing in one sentence as it does in another sentence, or the same thing that a different linguistic expression means in the same or a different sentence (synonomy) and; (3) when a linguistic expression's meaning is unclear in a given sentence because it could mean more than one thing in that sentence (ambiguity). My discussion of *sentential* meaning will utilize some recent work by J. Kress and myself (Kress & Odell, 1982) on the topic of multivocality and some very recent work of my own on the topics of synonymy and ambiguity. My explication of the notion of *contextual* meaning—the least tidy, if not more complicated, dimension of meaning—consists of: (1) an exposition of the contributions to our understanding of this topic in the writings of the major ordinary language philosophers: Wittgenstein, Waismann, Austin, and Strawson, to which I will add a point or two of my own; and (2) a formulation of these contributions as a set of principles governing natural language communication. In accomplishing the latter task, I will refine and make use of some earlier efforts of mine in this direction (Odell, 1981, 1984b).

I will begin, however, with some remarks of a general nature about interacting with and controlling others via language or what I have called "linguistic maneuvering." At the end of the paper I will speak about the more specific topic of linguistic manipulation and indicate how it can to some extent be offset.

LINGUISTIC MANEUVERING

There are a variety of means men use to gain power over others. Humans control other humans by use of arms, money, heredity, titular roles, religion, as well as democratic procedures. By these means, as well as others, we manipulate, force, control, coerce, persuade, and otherwise *get* others to do what we want them to do. The motivating forces are emotions, primarily: fear, love, hope, hate, and carnal desire. Human beings are not machines. They cannot be programmed to do what we want them to do, and I say this knowing full well that there are many believers in artificial intelligence who think otherwise. They are mistaken (Odell, 1981, 1984b). Humans have to be maneuvered via their emotions. Ultimately, our needs are the reins by which others control us. We all seek food, water, shelter, clothing, self-preservation, and sexual gratification, unless, of course, we are unconscious, live in a tropical climate, are suicidal, or eunuchs.

Fortunately, we are not *always* at the mercy of our needs. There is one notable exception. Humans, some of them, possess reason. Not everyone is subject to its force, but some are, and sometimes those who are, are persons in high places. The "power" or "voice" of reason is a force which has to be recognized and dealt with by any researcher interested in the analysis of power. This is not to deny, however, that the reason that reason is such a powerful force is any different, at least for the most part, from what it is in the case of money or arms. If we did not have the needs and the desires we have, it is hard to imagine us persuaded by any of these *means*. Often our reasoning with others takes the form of urging the other to recognize the consequences of his acting counter to our advice. The most universal and effective reason for not doing something is the recognition that doing it will bring about harm to one's self.

As long as humans have resided together there has been a struggle for domination by some individuals over others. Physical strength, arms, and the power of numbers have always effected the outcome of such struggles. Money is a more recent, but hardly less efficacious *power base*. Language is, however, nearly as old a *means* for getting others to do what one wants done as is physical force.

We often get others to do what we want by threatening them with something of the form, "If you don't _____, you will _____." How the blanks get filled in is multifarious and relativistic. What is perceived as a threat in one society or set of circumstances need not be so perceived in another society or a different set of circumstances. But there are some things which do have an almost universal force, such as, for example, the fear of death and the fear of severe and lasting pain for one's self or a loved one. There are, of course, as always, some exceptions to even this generalization. There is the man who wants to die or would have his loved ones die because he believes, like Jim Jones, that death is preferable to living on this planet. The existence of such fanatics does not, however, diminish in the slightest the force that the threat of death has for most of us most of the time. Few of us are able to laugh at death. Most of us are even more afraid of a prolonged but utterly painful existence. Of course it is the fear of death or a prolonged and painful existence which ultimately determines our behavior and not the threat of them. We are not really afraid of language as such, but rather what it promises. It is for this reason that I previously described language as a *means* for the control of others, rather than, as I did in the case of arms, as a *power base*.

Language must be viewed as having a *secondary* or *dependent* status in the kind of case I have been talking about. The same kind of effect could be achieved by raising one's sword arm, or even by a certain kind of look. There are, in spite of this, certain actions of a consequential sort, more closely woven into the fabric of language. Story telling accompanied by flamboyant gesture, novels, poems, plays, and even histories can be inspirational and result in actions which change whole societies. One cannot ignore the fact that Homer's epics inspired subsequent history. Alexander the Great was much inspired by them. For him they were accompanied by his mother Olympia's *claim* (necessitating language) that he was descended from the

Iliad's greatest hero, Achilles. The desire for honor and fame is certainly not a universal motivator, but what is interesting about it is how closely it is tied to linguistic actions. Here language plays a *primary* role. But it is not *independent* of all nonlinguistic factors.

Language also plays a primary role in such actions as praising. We can honor other human beings by building monuments or erecting statues in their memory, but praising another person is essentially a linguistic act.

Although fear of the consequences of disobedience as well as the desire to live in harmony with others play fundamental roles in and explain the force of the laws, language is of instrumental importance to their existence and perpetration. Language is the vehicle we use to express laws as well as their living record.

Language plays an important role in the education and daily existence of human beings. We use it to exhort, manipulate, convince, tempt, exonerate, excuse, warn, promise, avow, threaten, and punish. It is used as punishment when, for example, we call a child "bad," scold, censure, ridicule, or otherwise verbally belittle her in public.

The contribution of language to reasoning cannot be doubted, but even more noteworthy is the fact that without language certain abstract thoughts would be impossible. Descartes made use of this fact in his refutation of Hobbe's brand of empiricism. Wittgenstein reminds us of it when he asks us to contrast our saying certain things to ourselves with our thinking them but not saying them to ourselves. We can understand the point these philosophers were making if we say to ourselves that a million-sided polygon is a greater-sided one than a million-sided one minus four of its sides, and then try to think it without saying it to ourselves. And don't be mislead by the fact you can *image* a many-sided polygon being greater than another you image. The image of these two figures in your conceptual field is not nearly specific enough to capture the thought I asked you to have. The picture you imagine will fit just as well the thought that a thousand-sided polygon is a greater-sided one than is a thousand-sided one minus four of its sides. Such considerations as these clearly establish the impossibility of our doing certain things without language. If further evidence is needed in favor of this contention one need only ask how it is possible without language to make the case I just made for it. Establishing this does not, however, do much justice to the highly complex and intricate structure of natural language and its effectiveness. In what follows I will make up for this deficiency.

THE BASICS

Words are obviously among the basic elements of communication. So are phonemes, but I will refrain from saying anything about them. My analysis will not, and it need not, delve any deeper into the structure of language than the level of the word. We must distinguish, between (a) *word tokens,* which are the actual physical entities that one finds on the very page on which I type and which are different tokens than those on the page from which you read this, and (b) *word types,* which are the patterns one must utilize to, for example, count all the 'the's in a particular copy of this manuscript. They are what the mind must grasp if it is to recognize that 'minotaur,' 'minotaur,' and 'minotaur' are all physical expressions of the same thing, while at the same time recognizing that 'centaur,' and 'centaur' are both physical expressions of a different thing.

Sentences are composed of words and they are also subject to the *type/token* distinction. The physical sentences which compose my copy of Frege's collected papers are different from those making up anyone else's copy of it, but the types are the same.

Two sentences of different types can, however, have the *same* meaning. 'I speak German' and 'Ich spreche Deutsch' mean the same thing although they are different sentence types. And this is true even though the references of the words 'I' and 'Ich' may differ. I follow Strawson (1963) in maintaining that we must distinguish between the reference and the meaning of both words and sentences. I will follow tradition and use the word 'proposition' to refer to what these two sentences have in common, namely, their meaning.

Of paramount importance is the distinction which I mentioned in the beginning of this essay, namely, the distinction between what a given sentence *means,* which is a function of what its words mean, and what is *meant by* a given use of it, which is a function of the context of its utterance (Grice, 1965, 1969). The same sentence type can be used on various occasions to say very different things. What is *meant by* the sentence 'He is real bad' in the context of any even moderately hip high school setting is contradictory to what it can be said to *mean.* We must then distinguish between what a sentence means—a proposition, and what it can be used to mean—a *statement.* A statement is a sentence or a string of words used by a particular person on a particular occasion. Statements are not, however, the only uses to which sentences can be put. We can also use a given sentence to warn, command, and so on. I will say more about this aspect of language later. Moreover, we must recognize that one can succeed in making a statement without using a full declarative sentence. This is why I included the expression 'a string of words' in my definition of a statement.

Finally, there are *standard* and *nonstandard* uses of sentences. Some statements or uses of sentences correspond to what the sentence means and some do not. What this implies is that sometimes there is no significant difference between what a given sentence means and what someone meant by it. Or to put it somewhat differently, there are times when there is no important difference between what the words *mean* and what we *mean by* them. As I use the term, a *standard* use of a sentence is one where the words are used to mean what they *do* mean. If I say of someone with a certain sarcastic tone of voice, "He is very nice," I can succeed in saying that he is a perfect ass. This example illustrates very nicely what I mean by a *nonstandard* use of a sentence. Using 'He is a real bad man' as previously imagined is another example of a nonstandard use of a sentence.[1]

SENTENTIAL MEANING

One can imagine a sentence which in all probability has never been stated. The following is an example of such a sentence.

The pink pansy greeted Jack Odell and Theseus with a beckoning smile.

In spite of the fact that no one has ever made a statement with this sentence, we can ask about its meaning. If asked to explain what it means, we might well respond with something like:

The word 'the' picks out one individual as opposed to more than one, or as Bertrand Russell would have it, it means *one and only one*. 'Pink' is the word for a color derived from red by adding white to it. A pansy is a small flower which comes in a variety of shades. Greeting someone is a ceremonial welcoming of one person to another or others. Jack Odell is a professor of philosophy. Theseus is a Greek hero, sired by Poseidon. The phrase 'with a beckoning smile' modifies 'greeting.' It specifies how they were greeted. A smile is a facial expression involving the mouth, etc. A beckoning smile is a smile which, with the use of other facial expressions, for example, raising the eyebrows, indicates a come hither look or flirtatious invitation.

Now consider the following sentences:

Marilyn Monroe greeted Clark Gable with a seductive smile.
The Pink Panther said hello to Sam Spade.

The present Prime Minister of Greece may not be red but he sure is pink.

He fell of a bank.

With the exception of the second of these sentences, I have heard them all used in the making of statements. But we don't have to imagine a context of usage before we can determine: (a) what they mean; (b) if some of the words in one of them means the same as they do in others; (c) if a word in one of them means something different than it does in another; or (d) if some of the words in them are ambiguous. The 'greeted' of the first one means the same as it does in the sentence about a pink pansy, Theseus, and

---

[1] For more details regarding the basics, see Odell (1984c).

me. But it does not mean what it does in the third sentence. The last sentence is ambiguous because the word 'bank' is ambiguous in this sentential context. It is one thing to make these observations, it is quite another to demonstrate that they are true. This can only be done after criteria are provided for difference of sense or meaning (*multivocality*), sameness of sense (*synonymy*), and *ambiguity*. Making use of some recent work by J. Kress and myself (1982), I will proceed to provide a criterion for multivocality. Making use of some very recent work of my own (1984a), I will provide criteria for synonymy and ambiguity. By doing these things, I will clarify what these concepts mean and hence illuminate what is often left murky and obscure. Often, when people speak about the power of language they talk about multivocality, synonymy, and ambiguity, but they rarely specify exactly what it is they are talking about. For this reason, these discussions remain obscure, vague, and muddled. They are more or less useless. By doing what I am about to do, I hope to promote clear and productive research on the topic of the powers of language.

Multivocality, Synonymy, and Ambiguity

In "A Paraphrastic Criterion for Difference of Sense," J. Kress and I distinguished multivocality from ambiguity thus:

> *e* is *multivocal* in a language *L* if and only if *e* has a different sense in sentence S_1 than it has in S_2.
> *e* is *semantically ambiguous* in language *L* if and only if there are some sentences S_1, S_2, . . . in *L* which contain *e*, and within which *e* may be used in more than one sense, and the meaning (and truth conditions) of S_1, S_2, . . . varies depending upon the sense attributed to *e*. (pp. 183–184)

In a recent paper (1948a), I offered the following *prima facie* definitions of two different kinds of synonymy:

> An expression *e* in S_1 is *monotypically synonymous* with *e* in S_2 if *e* is used in the same sense in S_1 and S_2.
> An expression *e* in S_1 is *multitypically synonymous* with *f* in S_2 if *e* and *f* are used in the same sense. (p. 119)

The first kind is the kind of synonymy that holds between two tokens of the *same* type. The latter is the kind of synonymy that obtains between two tokens of *different* type.

We now possess definitions for the three fundamental parameters of sentential meaning. These definitions are, however, only superficially useful. A full-blown semantic theory must provide criteria for determining the presence within a natural language of instances of multivocality, synonymy, and ambiguity. I will now provide such criteria for each of these key notions.

I will begin with multivocality because I will be using the criterion for it in the formulation of the criteria for the others.

Multivocality

J. Kress and I (1982) have proposed the following criterion for multivocality:

> An expression e has a different sense in S_1 than it has in S_2 if: (1) there is a word or phrase f which is a metaphrase* of e in S_1; (2) there is a word or phrase g which is a metaphrase* of e in S_2; (3) there are no sentences in which either f or g is a metaphrase* of the other; and (4) neither S_1 nor S_2 is odd. (p. 191)

A *metaphrase* is simply a paraphrase or substitution instance which neither changes the truth value of the original sentence nor produces a sentence which is odd. An acceptable metaphrase must be both truth preserving and non-nonsense producing. A *metaphrase** is defined in terms of a metaphrase thus:

> An expression e is a metaphrase* of f in S_1, if and only if (i) e is a metaphrase of f in S_1; (ii) e is a metaphrase of f in each of S_2, S_3, ..., S_n such that among the set composed of S_2, S_3, ..., S_n there are: (a) various sentences having the same syntactic structure as S_1, but in which each of the expressions within S_1 other than f has been replaced by an expression very different in meaning from itself, and (b) sentences having various different syntactic structures from that of S_1.[2] (p. 191)

To see how the criterion works consider the following examples:

(S_1)   That substance in your hand is *honey*.
(S_2)   That girl is a real *honey*.

Honey in S_1 can be metaphrased* by *a sweet substance produced by bees*. *Honey* in S_2 can be metaphrased* by *a very pretty girl*. Moreover, *a sweet substance produced by bees* can be substituted for *honey* in each of a set of sentences having members of the same syntactic structure as S_1, but in which each of the expressions within S_1 other than f has been replaced by an expression very different from itself, for example:

(S_1')   My favorite spread is *honey*.
(S_2'')   The best ingredient in that cake is *honey*.

---

[2] This may seem unnecessarily complicated to the reader, but if he will consult "A Paraphrastic Criterion for Difference of Sense" (pp. 187–191), he will discover that there are cogent reasons for the complexity.

The following are examples of sentences which have a different syntactic structure than S_1, but in which *honey* can be replaced by *a sweet substance produced by bees* while preserving truth conditions.

(S_1''')   *Honey* is sold over the country in grocery stores.
(S_1'''')   I have never seen a dog who would eat *honey*.

Pretty girl can be substituted for *honey,* in accordance with condition (a) in, for example:

(S_2')   She was one *honey*.
(S_2'')   Her sister was some *honey*.

Condition (b) is satisfied by the following examples:

(S_2''')   I sure wish I knew how he got that *honey* to date him.
(S_2'''')   If I had known that that *honey* I met yesterday was going to be at your party, I wouldn't have missed it for the whole damn world.

And the substitution of *a sweet substance produced by bees* can replace *honey* in S_1 and *pretty girl* can replace *honey* in S_2 without change of truth value. Finally, there are no sentences in which *a sweet substance produced by bees* can metaphrase* *pretty girl,* and neither S_1 nor S_2 is odd.

Synonymy

There is an intimate connection between the concept of synonymy and the concept of metaphrasity*. With the use of the latter I have in "Paraphrastic Criteria for Synonymy and Ambiguity" (hereafter referred to as PCSA) proposed the following criteria for *monotypical* and *multitypical* synonymy.

> An expression *e* in S_1 is *monotypically synonymous* with *e* in S_2 if: (1) there is a word or phrase *f* which is a metaphrase* of *e* in both S_1 and S_2; (2) there is no word or phrase *g* which is a metaphrase* of *e* in S_1 but not in S_2; and (3) neither S_1 nor S_2 is odd.
>
> An expression *e* in S_1 is *multitypically synonymous* with *f* in S_2 if: (1) there is a word or phrase *g* which is a metaphrase* of *e* in S_1 and of *f* in S_2; (2) there is no word or phrase *h* which is a metaphrase* of *e* in S_1 but not of *f* in S_2; and (3) neither S_1 nor S_2 is odd. (p. 119)

The way these criteria work can be illustrated by use of the following sentences.

(A) Anita is *extremely mad at* me.
(B) I am *extremely mad at* that silly little impressionist painter.
(C) Erin is *furious with* me.

The 'extremely mad at' of (A) is monotypically synonymous with the 'extremely mad at' of (B) and it is multitypically synonymous with the 'furious with' of (C).

Ambiguity

Ambiguity is the most complex of the three parameters of meaning, and for that reason it is the hardest to define. It is a mistake to approach this topic by asking if ambiguity is a property of an expression or a property of a sentence. It makes no sense whatever to ask about an expression in isolation whether or not it is ambiguous. The ambiguity of an expression is a function of the sentential context in which it is found. Whether or not an utterance is ambiguous is a function of the context in which it occurs. *Sentential* ambiguity is a product of the meaning of the various words which make up the sentence. *Contextual* ambiguity is the result of lots of things, including body language, intonation contour, what was said before and after a given utterance, as well as the *background* of the utterance (which includes how well the auditor knows the speaker, how sophisticated the auditor is, whether he is being spoken to in his own language, and how much he knows regarding the topic of conversation). Contextual ambiguity cannot be formally defined. Instances of it are the result of a variety of factors none of which, nor even any subset of which, are always present. Sentential ambiguity can, however, as I have claimed in PCSA, be defined as:

> An expression e is *ambiguous* in S_1 if: (1) there are at least four words or phrases f, g, h, and i such that: (a) the addition of h to e in S_1 results in a sentence S_2, and (b) the addition of i to e in S_1 results in a sentence S_3, and (c) f is a metaphrase* of e/h in S_2, and (d) g is a metaphrase* of e/i in S_3; and (2) there are no sentences in which either f or g is a metaphrase* of the other; and (3) none of the sentences S_1, S_2, S_3, nor the sentences which result from metaphrasing* e/h or e/i by f and g respectively, are odd. (p. 122)

Words or expressions are ambiguous when they are found in sentential contexts which do not provide sufficient cues to make precise their meanings. Ambiguous expressions are expressions whose meanings are incomplete. A word or an expression can be said to be ambiguous when there are at least two different things it could mean and there is nothing about the sentence in which it is found which favors one of these meanings over the other.

To understand how the criterion works let us consider an ambiguous example, namely, 'He fell off a bank.' There is an expression 'river' which when added to the expression 'bank' produces the expression 'river bank' and another one, 'monetary,' which when added to the expression 'bank' yields 'monetary bank.' The former can be metaphrased* by 'mound of ground adjacent to and retaining a river,' and the latter by 'banking institution,' and neither of these expressions can metaphrase* the other in *any* sentential context. Moreover, while we would be unlikely to say of someone that he fell off a mound of ground adjacent to and retaining a river, it isn't odd in the relevant sense of 'odd.''

We are now in possession of criteria for determining with respect to sentential meaning when an expression is used in the same or a different sense as another expression, and when an expression's meaning is ambiguous. I will now turn to the topic of contextual meaning.

CONTEXTUAL MEANING

The contextual factors affecting meaning or meaningful discourse are multifarious. It would be extremely presumptious of me to pretend or talk as if the analysis I am about to propose is exhaustive, or even that it is exhaustive of all the significant aspects affecting meaningful discourse. Nevertheless, undaunted and armed with certain notions from the works of Wittgenstein, Waismann, Austin, Strawson, and drawing upon some previous work of my own on this subject, I will attempt to isolate and explicate a fairly extensive collection of contextual parameters involved in semantics and discourse analysis.

What someone *means by* something he or she says on some specific occasion, as opposed to what their words mean, is, in part, a function of *where* and *when* it was said. To say that she, or even that, say Helen, is clever, mean, sweet, and so on, is to say something which will sometimes mean or *refer to* one person, and will sometimes mean someone else. What a word means is—in one sense of the word 'means'—very different from what it means in the sense it has in, for example, 'I meant Schopenhauer not Mighty Mouse.' In this sentence what it means—can be metaphrased* by—*was referring to.* In many other linguistic contexts it means *word meaning,* for example, 'What does 'hedonism' mean?'

Referential words—whose primary function is to refer, words that are ordinarily classified as singularly referring expressions: proper names, pronouns, demonstratives, descriptions—are *essentially* context dependent. They are not ambiguous in spite of the fact that many philosophers—including Bertrand Russell—thought so. Their referents are usually quite clear, and this is because those contextual factors, the where and the when, function to secure their referents. It would be a mistake to think, however, that these two factors are the only relevant contextual variables. *How* something is said is just as important a determinant of meaning as is *where* and *when* it was said.

How something is said or its *intonation contour* can completely change the meaning of the words one uses. The sentence 'He is a real friend' means that whomever is referred to is someone on whom one can rely, but if one says it with a sarcastic inflection upon the word 'real,' one can say something contradictory to its meaning. With this inflection what one is saying is that the person referred to is anything but a person on whom one can rely. Where we place the emphasis or the intonation contour of what we say is not, however, the only factor relevant to an assessment of how something was said. The *body language* of the speaker, which includes such things as shoulder movement, hand gestures, mouth and eye movement, as well as other facial gestures, also plays an enormous role in meaningful communication. Raising one's eyebrows when one says that someone is a real friend can have the same effect as a sarcastic inflection.

There are a large number of other factors affecting what we mean by the things we say. Tipping my hat in Searle's (1979) direction I will lump them together and refer to them as *background factors*. Such things as whether or not the participants in a discourse episode know each other, are strangers, relatives, lovers; whether or not they had other conversations on the same topic; whether or not they have similar histories (including their levels of education and country of origin); whether or not they like or dislike each other, can greatly affect what is meant by the various things one says. One may well say of something a close friend has said something like "I know that he said that she was very nice, but what he meant, even though he said it in a perfectly serious tone of voice, was that she was a perfect bore."

It is also important that we recognize along with Austin (1962) just how many are the numbers of kinds of *speech action* which can be accomplished by the same sentence. The same sentence can be used in various circumstances to state, warn, request, acknowledge, promise, express one's emotions, and so on. Consider what I have said in defense of this claim elsewhere (Odell, 1981). If we consider a sentence from Austin, namely, 'There is a bull about to charge,' its various uses can be illustrated thus:

> If you and I are short-cutting our way across a pasture and I yell out the sentence displayed above, ['There is a bull about to charge.'] there is very little doubt in my mind concerning whether or not you would get the point of my outburst. If not, you are apt to get a rather different sort of point(s). . . . I have tried to *warn* you.
>
> If you and I are on our way to a bullfight at the *Plaza de Torros* and hear on the car radio an announcer use the displayed sentence, we will take him to be *making a statement* either true or false. . .

Once we arrive at the bullring, you, who are at your first bullfight and don't understand very well what is going on, may use the displayed sentence, with the appropriate emphasis or speech pattern to *request* information regarding what the bull is about to do.

Following your request, I can use the same sentence to *acknowledge* that you are correct in the assumption underlying your request.

If, however, you have been disappointed several times already and are fast approaching utter boredom accompanied by exasperation, you may seek further assurance and ask me if I promise what I have just acknowledged. You have provided a setting that allows me to accomplish what you desire (a *promise*) by simply asserting the displayed sentence while nodding my head affirmatively.

After a long and tedious afternoon, you have become totally exasperated with the whole "bloody" business. You jump up out of your seat, shrug your shoulders and assert the displayed sentence as you hurriedly seek the exit. You have clearly and quite unambiguously succeeded in *expressing your feelings* about bullfighting. You hate it!

These examples not only evidence the claim that the same sentence can be used in many different ways to express different meanings, but further exemplify my claim that what can be meant by a sentence is a function of *where, when* and *how* it is said. Continuing with what I said elsewhere (Odell, 1981):

> The meaning of the sentence in question changes depending upon whether it is said in a pasture, in an automobile or at the *Plaza de Toros*. It also depends on when it occurs. One cannot easily promise with it unless it has been *preceded by* a certain kind of event. Whether or not a given utterance of it is to be understood as a question, statement, etc., depends also on how it is said. When we wish to ask a question with it we must accent it a certain way. Accentuated a different way it will mean something else. (pp. 10–12)

The form that a string of words has need not be relevant to a determination of what someone meant by that string in some specific context. When a sergeant asserts the following string to a private, he is not, as its form suggests, asking a question, instead he is issuing an order.

Would you notify the first platoon of our departure(?)

We often use declaratives to ask questions or to issue commands, and we use questions to command and assert. These actions are often accomplished, as in the case of using the declarative sentence about the bull to *ask* if it is about to charge, by using a certain voice inflection or intonation contour.

In *Philosophical Investigations* Wittgenstein (1953) challenged the traditional view that what our words mean can be specified by a set of necessary and sufficient conditions. According to Carnap (1959), one has provided the necessary and sufficient conditions, and thus specified the meaning of, the word 'arthropod' when one has provided the necessary and sufficient conditions for the sentence 'x is an arthropod.' He further claims to have done so with:

a. x is an animal.
b. x has a segmented body.
c. x has jointed legs.

Wittgenstein's challenge to this view led to the *family resemblance* doctrine of meaning for empirical terms, which is explained by him in the often quoted passage from the *Investigations* concerning the word 'game' (p. 30). His point is that the various things which we call 'games' are so multifarious as to prohibit such characterization. There are board games, field games, card games, ball games, Olympic games, and so on. If one tries to list the necessary and sufficient conditions surrounding our use of this word as well as other empirical terms, we find we cannot because there is no one condition or set of conditions which they all have in common. Instead the conditions which are involved in our various uses of the term 'game' form "a complicated network of similarities overlapping and criss-crossing: sometimes overall similarities, sometimes similarities, sometimes similarities of detail. The various things we call 'games' like the members of a *family* share certain overlapping and criss-crossing features causing them to *resemble* one another, but there are no features which they all possess.

The philosopher Waisman (1960), following Wittgenstein, makes a similar but actually quite different point about general empirical terms. What Waismann claims is that providing the necessary and sufficient conditions for any empirical term is, in principle, impossible because they are all *open textured*. What he means by this is that with any empirical term we can always *imagine* a set of circumstances wherein we couldn't say whether or not the term applied. No matter how we refine our definitions, and no matter how many conditions we specify, we can always conceive of a set of circumstances (perform a *Gedankenexperiment*) which will cause us to have doubts as to whether or not the term in question applies. In the case of an arthropod one can, for example, imagine all three of the conditions which Carnap requires being satisfied for some creature at some time t_1, and also imagine that thing not being jointed legged at some time t_2. Is it or is it not an arthropod? Or is it an arthropod at time t_1 but not at t_2? Or is it a creature very much like an arthropod, but not really one? Or is it just a new species of an arthropod? Waismann's point is that we don't know what to say here, and so the meaning of the word in question cannot be fixed. If we possessed a set of necessary and sufficient conditions for the word 'arthropod,' its logic would be fixed and the word would have precise boundaries. This is not the case with the word 'arthropod,' and according to Waismann, it is also not the case for any empirical word, including even those words, like 'gold,' which have rigid scientific definitions.

Often *open texture* and *family resemblance* are confused. Sometimes they are even equated. This is a serious error. They are quite different. The family resemblant nature of words has to do with their actual *use,* whereas their open texturedness has to do with their logic. Whether or not Wittgenstein is right about the family resemblant nature of, for example, 'games,' is a matter which can be settled simply by looking at the way we use the word. Whether or not Waismann is right about open texture is a matter which has to be decided on the basis of a *Gedankenexperiment.* We don't have to imagine the world being any different than it is in order to determine whether or not Wittgenstein is right, but we *must* imagine the world to be different than it is in order to even grasp Waismann's point.

One problem which is apt to arise at this point is whether or not there is an irreconcilable breach between my views regarding meaning and those of Wittgenstein and Waismann. According to my view a synonym is a metaphrase,* and, according to Kress and me, an expression is a metaphrase* of another *if and only if* certain conditions are satisfied. Since an expression can only be a metaphrase* of another if these conditions are met, doesn't it follow that when these conditions are met the meaning of an expression, which is given by a synonym, is fixed? And, isn't this exactly what Wittgenstein and Waismann were denying?

The answer to this line of objection is clear in the case of Waismann, not so clear in the case of Wittgenstein. As far as the open textured nature of our empirical concepts is concerned, one can simply claim in defense of my views that I am only claiming what I claim for expressions as they are actually used. As long as the world continues to behave as it has in the past we can specify metaphrasity* and hence synonymy, but if it changes from time to time we would be unable to do so. Metaphrasity* is as contingent a condition of the actual world as are the laws of physics. Both are subject to the kind of skepticism which Waismann raises. This means, of course, that the semantic rules of natural languages are not logically necessary conditions and that there is no such thing as the logic of empirical terms.[3] This does not mean, however, that semantic rules are simply arbitrary. I maintain that they are contingent necessities of the same sort as the so-called *verification principle.* In "A Defensible Formulation of the Verification Principle" (1982) James Zartman and I argued that the verification principle is a *necessary presupposition* for the existence of a natural language. The same thing can be argued as regards most second order semantic rules, not that 'gold'

---

[3] If there are any terms with fixed meanings, they are nonempirical terms, for example, 'triangle.'

should mean gold, a first order rule, but that once we establish a semantic link between, for example, 'gold' and gold a certain consistency (fixedness) *must* be maintained, otherwise, communication is impossible.

Wittgenstein's family resemblance doctrine is more difficult to reconcile with my view. According to Wittgenstein, the meanings of words, not just what we mean by them, are not specifiable in terms of sets of necessary and sufficient conditions. Whereas, I am claiming that there are synonyms, and that synonymous expressions stand to one another in terms of the relation of equivalence. And, since one *could* claim to have provided the meaning of an expression when he has provided a synonym, am I not maintaining what amounts to an essentialist's theory of meaning? No, and for two reasons. In the first place I am not claiming that any word has one and only one meaning. I recognize that there are sets of expressions each of which can be said to be synonymous with any of the others. I haven't the faintest idea what *the* meaning of any empirical term would be. They all have more than one meaning. But more importantly, I have not claimed, in fact, I have denied even the possibility of defining words in isolation. My account of meaning involves the distinction between contextual and sentential meaning, and claims to find synonymy, multivocality, and ambiguity only *within* sentential contexts. I do not claim either to be able to tell one what the word 'game' means, or that there is a set of necessary and sufficient conditions which govern its use. I don't think it is possible for anyone to say what the word 'game' means, and I agree with Wittgenstein regarding its family resemblance nature. What I am claiming is that I can, with the use of the Kress/ Odell and Odell criteria, establish synonymy, multivocality, and ambiguity for expressions *within* sentential contexts.

Another aspect of language which any analysis of the contextual dimension of meaning must recognize is how extraordinarily flexible natural languages are, and how this flexibility allows for that most important of all features of language, namely, creativity. What would poets and novelists and journalists and even academics do if language were not as flexible as it is?

What makes one natural language user more interesting and captivating than another is his ability to use language in innovative and unique ways— ways no other has traversed.

When Sir Walter Raleigh asks, in poetry, for his "scallop-shell of Quiet," and his "staff of Faith", we acknowledge the sentiments he expresses. We know perfectly well what Thomas Hardy means at the beginning of *The Return of the Native* when he likens Egdon Heath to a human face and says:

The face of the heath by its mere complexion added half and hour to evening; it could in like manner retard the dawn, sadden noon, anticipate the frowning of storms scarcely generated, and intensify the opacity of a moonless midnight to a cause of shaking and dread.

And can anyone who has read the *Philosophical Investigations* ever forget Wittgenstein's many uses of metaphor, simile, and analogy to convince us, in a sudden stroke, of things, which because of their complexity, would otherwise have required pages to enumerate and justify? I have always been particularly fond of his use of the simile concerning the "repair of a torn spider's web with our fingers" as a means of persuade us of the misconceptions we have concerning the desirability of ideal (formal) languages. And there is the sports reporter's reference to the recently revitalized New York Jets football team's onslaught on an opposing team as "Scrooge going after a nickle."

Who among us can resist the temptation to pun on occasion? I like the one on the wall of my favorite campus bar—I mean, pub. It is, "Smoking causes cancer, but it cures ham."

Not every creative use of language is easily catalogued. There are an enormous number of different kinds of things that one can accomplish when one uses a natural language. Consider the following graffito, "I'd rather have a bottle in front of me than a frontal lobotomy." And consider what I tried to accomplish above when I let it be known that I had a favorite bar, and then expressed my reluctance to have my haunt so described. It is a peculiar fact about language, ultimately about the very different kinds of places where alcohol is sold, that the description 'pub' is more honorous than 'bar.'

When I enumerated and exemplified some of the speech acts one could accomplish with the sentence 'There is a bull about to charge,' I included in that set the use of it to express one's emotions. We do this kind of thing daily. We are always talking about our joys, pains, fears, hopes, apprehensions, desires, pleasures, discomforts, and so on. And when we are insincere, we don't feel what we say we do feel. In those cases we are said to be lying. In order for me to express genuine concern, I must actually feel concern. There is all the difference in the world between saying I feel sorry for someone when I do, in fact, feel sorry for him and saying I do when I don't. Most of us not only appreciate such differences we often also *know* when someone else is being insincere.

When we use language in these various ways we intend to: amuse, annoy, convince, persuade, irritate, perplex, entertain, give rise to aesthetic experiences, etc., all of which are, to use an expression from J.L. Austin (1962), *perlocutionary* consequences of our speech actions. Sometimes the primary intentional objective of a speech action is, to use another expression from Austin, its *illocutionary* force. An example of this would be using the sentence concerning the bull who is about to charge as a promise. Promising, like all other conventional speech acts, is, according to Austin, an illocutionary action. But at other times the primary motive for some utterance is perlocutionary. We often use language with the intention to deceive, which is, of course, to use it to perform a perlocution. A soft-hearted lawyer may, for example, respond to his client's inquiry regarding whether or not the Governor is going to commute his death sentence with, "It's possible", when the lawyer knows that this particular governor has no intention whatever of commuting (an illocution) this particular prisoner's sentence. And he can do so with a modicum of impunity on the grounds that what he has said is true insofar as it is possible *for* any governor to commute any prisoner's sentence. The lawyer has taken advantage of an ambiguity surrounding the word 'possible.' What the lawyer said could mean either "It's possible *that* the Governor will commute your sentence." or "It's possible *for* the Governor to commute your sentence."

The kind of linguistic activity exemplified by the lawyer case comprises a considerable amount of our ordinary talk, and can only take place among emotional equals. The point of making jokes, expressing sarcasms, twisting language, devising poems, and so on, is to affect other's emotions. Unless the other has these emotions or feelings such communication with him is impossible.

The last observation I want to make about how natural languages are used is that the definition of one word always involves other words, which in turn, involve still others. No word in a natural language can be understood in isolation from *all* other words and ultimately from *most* other words. Elsewhere (Odell, 1981) I have attempted to explicate this point by the use of an analogy. I said:

> A word in a natural language is like a piece from a jigsaw puzzle. The role of any individual piece can be grasped only in the context of the complete puzzle. Without the rest of the pieces a given piece is meaningless because it has no purpose or function. "But couldn't it be given a purpose or function?" One could, of course, drill a hole through it, run a string through the hole and use it as a necklace. But then it is no longer functioning as it was *meant* to function. Strictly speaking, it is no longer a jigsaw puzzle piece, even though one might recognize it as such and so describe it. A word in a natural language, like a piece from a jigsaw puzzle, loses its function and its meaning when it is separated from all the other words (pieces) which comprise the language (puzzle). (p. 27)

What I have attempted to establish in this section can be summarized in terms of a set of principles governing the way we use natural language. This present set, which also appears in Odell (1984b), is a revised, updated, and extended version of an earlier attempt of mine in the same direction (Odell, 1981).

1. Communication through a natural language is, in large part, a function of context. *Where* and *when* something is said largely determines what was *meant by* what was said. (*context principle*)

2. What is *meant by* what we say is also a function of *how* we say it. Where or upon what word or words we place an emphasis (intonation contour), as well as how we move various parts of our bodies (body language), will frequently affect what we mean. (*emphasis principle*)

3. What is *meant by* what we say is also a function of the relationship we have to one another, how much knowledge the various participants in a given speech episode share, whether or not the participants have had previous conversations on the topic under consideration, what has taken place earlier in the given speech episode, etc. (*background principle*)

4. The range of things (speech acts) a given sentence can be used to accomplish is limitless. (*Multiple Speech Acts Principle*)

5. What a sentence *means* (a proposition) is often quite different from what we mean by it, which is sometimes a statement, sometimes a warning, sometimes a request, and sometimes something else. (*Intentionality Principle*)

6. What a given string of words means is not a function of the formal characteristics those strings possess. "Why not?" can be used to make a request, even though its *form* is that of a question. (*Non-Functionality Principle*)

7. The meaning of a great many speech acts is intentionally creative and nonstandard. We often use language in inventive and innovative ways to amuse, clarify, convince, annoy, insult, etc. Punning, poetry, word play, and pre-eminent prose all depend on our ability to use language with a certain impunity. (*Creativity principle*)

8. What most, if not all, general empirical terms *mean* in a natural language as, opposed to what we might *mean by* them on some specific occasion, cannot be specified formally, that is, in terms of necessary and sufficient conditions. They are family resemblant in nature. (*Family Resemblance Principle*)

9. Since most of the general empirical terms of a natural language are family resemblant in nature, it follows that in order to get at their meaning, i.e., the concepts they express, one must specify the set of overlapping and criss-crossing characteristics which determine the similarities and differences relevant to the question of whether or not some imagined or existing case falls under the concept in question. (*Overlapping and Criss-crossing Definitions Principle*)

10. Even if we legislate sets of necessary and sufficient conditions to govern what they mean, we can't be sure that our legislations will preclude the existence of contexts where we will be uncertain what our words mean, that is, we can still imagine cases where we wouldn't know whether or not a given word applied. The words of natural language are open textured. (*Open Texture Principle*)

11. The concept expressed by any given word in a natural language is in-extricably tied to the concepts expressed by nearly every other word in the language. While the words themselves are no doubt *discrete,* the concepts they involve, or are tied to, are *continuous* with other con-cepts. (*Continuity Principle*)

12. A very large number of speech acts which can be implemented in a natural language involve expressing one's emotions. A natural lan-guage incorporates the distinction between a genuine and a nongenu-ine expression of an emotion. Expressing concern, and expressing genuine concern are recognizably quite different. (*Sincerity Principle*) (Odell, 1984b pp. 137-139)

CONCLUSION

One of the more obvious conclusions to be drawn from a consideration of the last two sections is that what someone actually means when he or she uses language is much more likely to turn on contextual factors than on what their words can be demonstrated to mean. Still, if one is aware of all this he or she can prevent misunderstanding and force the other to be more careful to say exactly what it is he or she wishes to say. In other words, one can, if one possesses the power which this knowledge bestows, *force* the other to use language which says or means what the other wants to say. Much confusion can be avoided in this way, but more importantly, such power makes one immune to most forms of linguistic manipulation. The reason lawyers are able to get away with the things they get away with is because few of their clients possess more than a modicum of linguistic infor-mation of the sort which this paper has attempted to convey.

Armed with a thorough understanding of the basic variables contributing to linguistic maneuvering one can provide a coherent, cohesive, and more or less complete account of any linguistic episode. If that episode involves lin-guistic manipulation, one is in a position to demonstrate that it does. This in itself is an instantiation of linguistic power. All theoretical considerations or applications of theory to any subject matter, including language, is a second order linguistic activity, and is, as such, an exercise in linguistic power.

Sentential ambiguity results, according to my account, because we are not explicit enough regarding the things we say. Such ambiguity can be avoided, and the kind of linguistic manipulation which is its result can be offset. All we have to do is insist that others be more precise and explicit when they talk. No person can manipulate another the way lawyers do if the other sticks by his guns and insists that the would-be manipulator express himself unambiguously. This same procedure can also serve to *disambiguate* *contextual* ambiguities. One will find himself hard-pressed to hide behind ambiguity if the person he is discoursing with insists that he make precise his comments. The way to educate people to avoid being manipulated through discourse is to educate them semantically. If one has any doubts about this let him or her try to verbally gain the upper hand with an analytically trained philosopher or student of philosophy and logic. Verbal skills provide the only defense against another's linguistic onslaught. This paper is, among other things, an attempt to provide the foundations for the development of such skills.

REFERENCES

Austin, J.L. (1962). *How to do things with words.* Cambridge, MA: Harvard University Press.

Carnap, R. (1959). The elimination of metaphysics through logical analysis of language. In A.J. Ayer (Ed.), *Logical positivism.* New York: The Free Press.

Grice, H.P. (1969). Meaning. In T. Olshewsky (Ed.), *Problems in the philosophy of language.* New York: Holt Rinehart and Winston.

Grice, H.P. (1965). The causal theory of perception. In R.J. Swartz (Ed.), *Perceiving, sensing and knowing.* Garden City, NY: Doubleday.

Kress, J., & Odell, S.J. (1982). A paraphrastic criterion for difference of sense. *Theoretical Linguistics, 9,* 181–201.

Odell, S.J. (1981). *Are natural language interfaces possible?* (IBM systems research institute Technical Report # TR 73-024). New York.

Odell, S.J. (1984a). Paraphrastic criteria for synonymy & ambiguity. *Theoretical Linguistics, 11* (1/2), 117–125.

Odell, S.J. (1984b). On the Possibility of Natural Language Processing. *Theoretical Linguistics, 11* (1/2), 127–146.

Odell, S.J. (1984c). Paraphastic theory of meaning. *Theoretical Linguistics, 11* (3), 215–249.

Odell, S.J., & Zartman, J.F. (1982). A defensible formulation of the verification principle. *Metaphilosophy, 13,* 65–74.

Searle, J. (1979). Literal Meaning. In *Expression and Meaning.* Cambridge: Cambridge University Press: 117–136.

Strawson, P.F. (1963). On referring. In C.E. Caton (Ed.), *Philosophy and ordinary language.* Urbana, IL: University of Illinois Press.

Waismann, F. (1960). Verifiability. In A.G.N. Flew (Ed.), *Logic and Language.* Oxford: Basil Blackwell.

Wittgenstein, L. (1953). *The philosophical investigations.* New York: Macmillan.

Part II

THE LANGUAGE OF COERCION

Chapter 4

Conversational Power in FBI Covert Tape Recordings

Roger W. Shuy
Georgetown University

Power is a matter of unequal balance, with one side *over*balanced in one direction and the other side *under*balanced in that direction. Power imbalances in language stem from a number of sources, including a person's ability with the language itself, his social status in relation to the other person, constraints imposed by the topic, age differences, and many others. These obvious linguistic and social imbalances, however, are not the focus of this paper. Instead, we begin with a highly recurring event in our society today: the surreptitious tape recording of conversations, done by the FBI or other government agencies, for the purpose of capturing evidence of wrongdoing in language.

Such a context produces a number of types of language power which are not traditionally observed. This is not to say that this power is unique to surreptitious tapes but, rather, that this power is clearly evident here. One reason that it is evident is that this power is so one-sided in this type of conversation.

Each year the FBI engages in covert operations in which conversations are recorded surreptitiously with suspected targets. In 1981, over 1300 such cases were carried out in New Jersey alone. Such conversations are not normal for many reasons. Especially abnormal is the power relationship which, in normal conversation, is either negotiated by strength of argumentation and evidence, or is dictated by obvious status indicators.

Central to the assymetry of power in covert recordings are two factors. The first factor lies in the hidden purpose of the covert recorder which is to capture illegal speech acts (language crimes) on tape such as promises, offers, admissions of past guilt, or conspiracy. The ostensible purpose of the covert recorder, of course, is quite different. It is deliberately misrepresented as a perfectly legal goal. The result is a conversation in which there is a hidden agenda which has power over the target's freedom, equivalent to a secret weapon in international warfare. The second factor central to the assymetry of power is that of *time* and *audience*. The covert recorder is making a tape to be listened to by a later audience, a jury in particular. Since the FBI agent knows this, he can direct the conversation toward that purpose. Examination of over a thousand hours of FBI-produced surreptitious audio and video recordings reveals a number of conversational strategies commonly used by the government agents, including the following: well-timed interruptions which block the target from making exculpatory statements, the agent's conversion of legal words used by the target into illegal words, isolating the target from information which he needs to respond legally and clearly, using ambiguity to work for the prosecution of the target, and making it appear that the government has achieved illegal agreement on issues for which no such agreement actually has been accomplished.

The target, not knowing that he is being recorded, tends to treat the conversation like any normal conversation. Had he known he was being recorded, for example, he would request clarification more persistently when ambiguity exists rather that letting unclear statements go by unchallenged, as we all often do in everyday talk.

All speakers have strategies for advancing their own agendas and, conversely, for ignoring, blocking, or thwarting the agendas of others, especially those agendas with which they are not comfortable. It is in this area of conversational strategies, especially strategies which block the agendas of the other speaker, where recent government practice causes concern. The seven types of conversational power which are evident in these tapes are as follows:

1. The power of known conversational significance
2. The power of controlled agenda
3. The power of camouflaged agenda
4. The power of created atmosphere
5. The power of blocked agenda
6. The power of conversational isolation
7. The power of deliberately unclear language use

THE POWER OF CONVERSATIONAL SIGNIFICANCE

Since the target in an FBI scam does not know that he is being tape recorded, his use of the normal conversational feedback utterances such as *uh-huh, yeah, alright, OK,* and so on can be taken, by a later listener, such as a jury, as evidence of agreement with what the agent is saying, even though feedback markers such as these are not necessarily indicators of agreement.

Conversations taped by the government contain hundreds and hundreds of examples of such speaker responses, especially in telephone conversations where the need to let the other person know that you are still there is even more crucial. Even though these do not signify agreement, prosecutors, courts, and juries often confuse such lax tokens with positive agreement. To some this may not be considered a problem for which the prosecution should be concerned. I disagree. If an indictment is made on the basis of a presumed agreement when, in fact, the response meant "I hear you, keep talking," a false indictment has been made.

The point of this argument is simple. In matters involving guilt or innocence, the jury should be certain that the target's response is a full token "I agree," "That's right," "I'm with you," or "You have my agreement," "It's a deal," or even "Yes" followed by another positive marker such as "Yes, of course," or "Yes, that's right." To be completely unambiguous in what the target means, a true positive response must be obtained. But what advantage is there to the government to elicit false indicators of agreement such as lax tokens? The power position of the FBI in the taping event is that they know that later listeners will take these lax tokens as agreement markers. The recording agents know that the conversation is being taped and they know that the jury will hear the *uh-huh* as agreement. This would not be evidence of power in itself if it were not that the obverse were also true. The target does not know that he is being recorded and is, therefore, not careful to avoid the *appearance* of agreement and he is not careful to disambiguate simple conversational feedback indicators (which mean "I hear you," "I understand what you're saying," or even "I don't necessarily agree but I'll hear you out" from simple signals of agreement. The power of the government agent is in the potential ambiguity which results from the confusion between positivity and agreement. Lax tokens are positive but not consensual.

Since the government has the power of knowing the conversational significance and the target does not, the target is not in a position to know that his lax tokens can be taken as agreement. In the same manner, the target is not as apt to request clarification when he does not understand because, in everyday conversation, we often let unclear statements go by in the vague hope that eventually things will get clearer. If the target only knew that the agent's ambiguity, in such instances, could work against him, he might well choose to request clarification on the spot.

THE POWER OF CONTROLLED AGENDA

A second area of language power which has been used by the FBI in criminal investigations is that of coaching the target in what to say in a crucial conversation. The Abscam case of Senator Harrison A. Williams, Jr. contains a classic example of FBI coaching to the target to say what the agents want him to say. On June 28, 1979, the convicted criminal hired by the FBI, Mel Weinberg, gave the Senator 28 directives about what he should say in his meeting with the presumed Arab sheik immediately following. Senator Williams believed that this follow-up meeting was to be about obtaining a loan from the wealthy sheik. Weinberg's agenda, quite the contrary, was to get the Senator to "blow his own horn" on tape, to create the atmosphere of greed and illegality. The directives which Weinberg made to Williams in the coaching session are listed on the left hand column of Figure 1. The three columns on the right then demonstrate who actually introduced these directives in the follow-up meeting with the sheik.

It is clear from the chart that when Weinberg's directives were introduced, when the coaching was actually brought into practice, it was agents

FIGURE 1.   The Coaching of Senator Williams

Weinberg's Coaching Topics	Topics Introduced in Following Meeting by		
	Errichetti	FBI Agent DeVito	Williams
how high you are	X	X	
fifth in Senate	X	X	
who do you know		X	
chairman of whatever	X		
how important	X		
without you there is no deal	X		
you put this together		X	
get government contracts	X		
how important	X	X	
influence for contracts	X	X	
important	X	X	
how important you are	X	X	
who you are	X	X	
without me, no deal	X	X	
I'm the man[a]			
open doors		X	
use influence	X	X	
I guarantee this	X		
we'll produce		X	
blow your own horn	X	X	
who you control		X	
I can move this		X	
I guarantee this	X		
sell him like mad	X	X	
you're the boss		X	
I'm the power		X	
throw names	X		
come on strong	X	X	

[a] Not brought up by anyone.

Tony DeVito and co-opted conspirator Angelo Errichetti, and *not* Senator Williams, who did so. Keep in mind here that topic introduction is the key to intentions or conversational agendas. It is true that Senator Williams did say, on that tape, that the Vice President used to work on his committee and that Secretary Vance was a neighbor of his in New Jersey, but these statements were not topic *initiations*. They were made in *response* to questions asked him about officials that he knew. Responses are quite different from initiations. If asked a question, a person has the obligation to answer, but this answer is not a strong indication of intention, or agenda. Senator Williams does *not* initiate topics about how important he is or whom he knows. He does *not* specify, as coached, that without him there is no deal or that he is the man that opens doors. He does *not* say whom he controls, what he moves, or that he's the boss. He does *not* sell like mad or blow his own horn. Senator Williams' statements can be considered nothing short of a failure at self-promotion. In fact, he actually violated Weinberg's coaching and introduced the one topic which Weinberg had said *not* to bring up, the mining venture itself.

Power, in this case, involves control of the agenda. The target, Senator Williams, was rendered powerless both in the coaching session and in the follow-up meeting with the sheik. His agenda was the mine. He was told not to bring it up. He brought it up anyway, but was overpowered by agent DeVito and co-opted conspirator Errichetti, who introduced the "horn blowing" topics on his behalf.

Another important point should be made about the coaching strategy. Not only were concepts suggested, as Figure 1 indicates, but actual *scripting* was used by Weinberg. By scripting I refer to when Weinberg and Errichetti change their *you* references to actual modeling sentences, as follows:

MW: Without *me* there is no government contracts.
MW: Without *me* there is no deal.
MW: *I'm* the man.
MW: Use *my* influence.
MW: *I* guarantee this.
AE: And *we'll* produce.
AE: *I* can move this.
AE: *I* can move that.
AE: *I* guarantee this.
AE: *I* can do that.

This change from *suggestion* of what Senator Williams should say to the sheik to the *actual sentences* he should use becomes what in the field of education is called directed teaching; putting words in the mouth of students whether or not they want to say them.

Coaching is the equivalent of a leading question; question probing in any area of activity grows more dangerous as it predetermines the results. In police investigation, for example, the fact value of the answer to what linguistics call a tag question, is minimal. Figure 2 illustrates a continuum of fact value dependant on the type of question asked. By coaching the target to say what the agent wants him to say, the FBI gets low fact value, if any at all.

The ultimate effect of this assymetry of conversational power is, of course, on the later listener, the jury in particular.

Those who listen to recordings of people talking tend to overgeneralize many things. For example, if one listens to a conversation between two people, one of whom is swearing and the other of whom is not, the general impression that the third party listener gets is that *both* are swearing. This is what I refer to as the *contamination principle*. There are many dangers of contamination in FBI covert recordings. In the case of Senator Williams, the fact that *none* of the horn-blowing topics were generated by the Senator seems not to have been noticed by the jury or even by the U.S. Senate itself. Yet the facts of the actual tapes are clear. The power of the government, therefore, is in creating an illusion through language, in this case through coaching and scripting, that Senator Williams had said things that, in fact, the agents had said themselves.

THE POWER OF CAMOUFLAGED AGENDA

This assymetry of conversational power is also demonstrated in the very nature of the scam operation. The press and even the court itself regularly confuse a sting operation with a scam. Stings begin in the context of an illegal operation in which a target's predisposition to buy stolen goods from a fencing operation or to purchase illegal drugs can be made relatively clear. A scam, in sharp contrast, begins in the context of an innocent, legal act. One may wonder, in fact, if even the title of Mel Weinberg's ghosted book,

FIGURE 2.

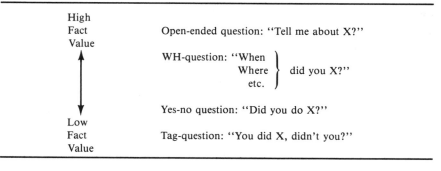

High
Fact   Open-ended question: "Tell me about X?"
Value

WH-question: "When
              Where } did you X?"
              etc.

Yes-no question: "Did you do X?"

Low
Fact   Tag-question: "You did X, didn't you?"
Value

Green's *The Sting Man* (Ballentine, 1981), was not an effort to promote the confusion between a sting and a scam which seems so prevalent today. Scams are camouflaged operations which are introduced with the appearance of legality. The power relationship in scam operations clearly works to favor the prosecution. The real agenda of the agents can be only one thing: to capture on tape illegal acts or words of the target. Otherwise there would be no reason for engaging in such an enterprise at all. In a sting operation, the illegal intention is made clear from the outset and an illegal act is performed when the target enters the scheme at all. A scam has to build up to the illegality from a legal beginning point. Thus, the target is presented with perfectly legal entry points such as a request to a public official to sponsor legislation of a foreign dignitary (as in Abscam) or the offer of saving the state a lot of money by rebidding state insurance (as in Texas Brilab). The government's power comes with its control by means of a hidden agenda. The substantive topic of conversation is desirable and legal, an enticement that can only be attractive to the official target who, by agreeing, would be doing nothing more than what his job requires him to do anyway.

Thus, when the illegal act is eventually proposed, the target is invariably off guard. In the case of Senator Williams, a bribe was offered in order to insure his support for the legislation. The Senator clearly rejected the bribe offer. In the case of Speaker of the Texas House, Bill Clayton, a campaign contribution was redefined, after it was given as a campaign contribution, as a bribe. Figure 3 displays the crucial sequence of this conversation.

FIGURE 3. Camouflaging in Brilab

Insurance Proposal	Campaign Contribution	Offer to Split Commission	Bill Clayton's Responses
JH: saving the state a million dollars			I'm for saving the state money.
	LM: We want to make a campaign contribution.		Let's take care of the insurance matter.
	LM: But could I, LM, knowing you all these years, make a campaign contribution?		Oh sure.
	LM: We will, I will, put in $100,000 and up to half a million.		My job is to try to save the state money.
		JH: There's $600,000 every year. I'm keeping 600 and 600 for you.	We don't want to do anything illegal and and you don't either.

The camouflage strategy is a common one in government taping. It clearly
violates the statement by Philip B. Heymann, Assistant Attorney General,
when he said:

> In the elaborate review process which Judge Webster has described, the Bureau
> and Criminal Division strive to insure that each undercover operation is carried
> out in a manner which is *fair, unambiguous,* productive of successful prosecu-
> tions and which minimizes the impact on or even the involvement with inno-
> cent persons. (*FBI Undercover Operations,* 1984, p. 36)

The camouflage strategy is not unambiguous. In contrast, it thrives on deliberate, created ambiguity and confusion. As such it violates the FBI's own
guidelines, but it certainly is a powerful tool to help convict targets.

THE POWER OF CREATED ATMOSPHERE

The fourth type of conversational power which the FBI utilizes in tape cases
is the ability to create whatever atmosphere it wants as part of the evidenciary record. It has been suspected that it is not accidental that Abscam
videotapes are black and white with poor resolution, angle, and focus. A
high tone hotel is made to appear to be a sleazy flophouse, for example.
Crucial passages of the target's speech are taped when the camera is focused
on the agents rather than the speaker. Despite the expensive recording equipment used by the government, the sound quality is regularly so bad that
nothing can be identified with certainty. Videotaped segments are sequenced
in such a way, as in the Abscam case of Congressman John Murphy, that
clearly illegal statements made to the agent by coopted conspirator Howard
Criden appear immediately before an exculpatory conversation between
that same agent and Murphy. The special effects of juxtaposition have been
long recognized in the film-making business.
    One language form of atmosphere creation can be discovered in virtually
all government covert recordings. Elsewhere I refer to this as the strategy of
criminalizing (Shuy, 1982). By criminalizing I mean the translation of perfectly legal terms and concepts used by the designated target into terms and
concepts which are illegal or covert. One of the charges against Senator
Williams, for example, is that he hid his interest in the proposed mining
business. The recorded conversation, however, makes it very clear that the
government agents' agenda to get him to adopt their covert terms and concepts failed completely. Figure 4 illustrates the contrast between the terms
used by Senator Williams (a legal *blind trust, go public, declare*) and the
words used by agents DeVito and Weinberg (*hidden, hide, secret, gimmick,*
and *some other way*).

FIGURE 4.   Senator Williams Blind Trust v. Hidden Interest

August 5
- MW: Keep it *secret, protect you,* 100% *protection.*
- TD: You *protected,* your position *protected,* everybody *protected.*

September 11
- HW: Right, *pay the taxes.*

October 7
- MW: Sandy spoke about you going to declare 17 million dollars *profit* or something.
- HW: No....I'm going to find a way to protect myself with some kind of *declaration.* I'm going to have to *go public* with something or other.
- TD: ...everything was going to be *hidden.*
- TD: Everybody can declare...*you can't.*
- HW: Well this is where the lawyer comes in Alex...we can *blind trust* me you know.

October 7
- TD: ...you were gonna declare it, but *some other way.*
- HW: ...now if it's a *blind trust*...that's the way for my purposes.
- TD: ...I said when the Senator said he wanted to declare...he was trying to *protect himself*...by coming up with some *gimmick.*
- HW: Well there we have it under the *trust*...so I've done what I had to do.

It is one thing to suggest illegal actions, but quite a different matter to attempt to convert legal intentions into illegal ones. The contamination effect had been produced, however, and both the court and the Senate Ethics Committee were somehow able to overlook what was actually said in favor of an interpretation which ignores Senator Williams' statements and highlights those of agents Weinberg and DeVito, even though these were denied and rejected by the Senator. In court cases involving tape recorded evidence, the contamination effect on later listeners of the illegal words or concepts of the agents can be devastating.

The creation of an illegal atmosphere, whether through the recording process itself or through the agents' translation of the target's words into illegal concepts and terms, is still another indication of the assymetrical power relationship in such conversations.

THE POWER OF THE BLOCKED AGENDA

We have already discussed the government's power to control the agenda and the power to camouflage their own hidden agenda. Agenda power has one more facet: the power to block the agenda of the target.

All conversations, in one sense or another, can become a kind of verbal warfare. Each participant can have a goal, or agenda, which he or she wishes to put forth. The extent to which this agenda is crucial can determine the strategies used to promote it. Some conversationists are aggressive enough to interrupt the other party's effort to promote his or her agenda. Government covert recordings show frequent evidence of this. Such blocking is particularly critical when the target is attempting to offer an exculpatory statement. When it is apparent that the target is about to reject or deny an illegal presentation, the agent regularly interrupts the target, either with words or, as in several Abscam cases, with the telephone. Telephone interruption was possible in Abscam because Special Agent Thomas Good was in the room adjacent to the videotaped room, monitoring and directing the operation. When he could see that things were not going well he could telephone the interviewing agent with new instructions or suggestions and, at the same time, block the target's denial or rejection.

We all interrupt for various reasons and, because of this, it may seem innocuous and unimportant. It is not the act of interrupting which is dangerous here; it is the *timing* of the interruption. In the tape recorded evidence used in the Abscam cases of Congressman Richard Kelly and Senator Harrison Williams, for example, the blocked exculpatory statement strategy is worthy of examination. Congressman Kelly was interrupted over and over again as he verbally rejected the offer of money three times directly and six more times indirectly (this, in itself, poses an important question to the government: How many times must a target reject the offer before the pursuit is called off?). Both in the Kelly and the Williams cases, however, still another blocked exculpatory statement approach is used: the telephone. The pattern of telephone interruptions in these cases is for the interruption to come at points which are activity peaks, ones in which the current government strategy has failed and it appears that a change in strategy is called for. In the case of Senator Williams, in his January 15, 1980 tape, the first telephone interruption blocks his effort to explain to the sheik why he was rejecting his offer of money. The Senator says *no* four times and then the telephone interrupts. The second telephone interruption comes a few minutes later after the Senator was trying to re-establish the reason he had agreed to meet the sheik in the first place: to represent the potential mining business' concerns. After the interruption, the sheik changes his agenda from offering money (which had failed) to an attempt to link this proposed loan to the mining business with securing the Senator's offer to sponsor legislation which would bring him into the country.

The assymetry of power in such conversations should be obvious. The target has considerably less power than the agents, largely because the government has the additional weapon of the well-timed telephone call. Likewise, the agents have the social power, largely because they are the ones who are offering the desirable commodity: the loan for American businessmen (as in the Williams case) and the opportunity to secure foreign investments in the politician's districts (as in the Murphy and Kelly cases). Add to this the fact that elected officials have learned to walk the middle road, to not overact, in essence, to be political and polite. The government made good use of such training and called on the power of the blocked agenda over and over again.

THE POWER OF CONVERSATIONAL ISOLATION

In everyday conversation, one normally has the ability to pick the people with whom one wants to talk. In covert operations, such as Abscam or Brilab, however, the government carefully orchestrates who will talk with whom and when. In doing so, it has the opportunity to keep certain information from the targets that they are trying to get, and thus they end up implicating themselves on tape. If some of the other targets have been, or appear to have been, already coopted, the strategy leans heavily on obtaining peer pressure to go along with what the others seem to want. Topic analysis and response analysis, two linguistic discourse tools, can clearly point out how much of an *outsider* the targets are in their conversations. In the case of Senator Williams, for example, there were many meetings between the government agents and targets other than the Senator. The topics discussed and the way they were discussed were substantially different when the Senator was not present from when he was. His role in the few conversations in which he *did* participate clearly displays that of an "outsider" who is trying to determine what was going on. Sixty percent of the topics Senator Williams introduced were requests for information. When a speaker spends almost two-thirds of his time trying to find out things that the others already know, he is clearly an "outsider" to the conversation.

The isolation strategy is used commonly in government recorded communications. It was used widely in the Brilab cases to insure that certain targets were kept ignorant of things that other co-opted participants already knew. The significance of the strategy is obvious. When the target is an "outsider," the already co-opted "insiders" can help the agents convince the target to perform the desired act. The peer pressure of friends and acquaintances is great. The desire not to appear ignorant or belligerent to an event which the others may have agreed to tends to cause the targets to "go along" with something about which they may know very little. The danger, of course, is that the target, even though unwilling to do or say the act, will be trapped into agreeing to do it anyway, not because he is predisposed to do so, or because he intends to do so, but purely from social pressure, or from the false assumption that his "insider" friends have done the proper investigating and thinking about an issue about which he is still ill-informed. For any of these reasons, the target may be captured on tape committing a language crime, that is making a promise or agreeing to do something which he does not fully understand even though his intention would be *not* to do so if he only had sufficient information. The government's power in such instances comes from its control over who will be the participants in any given conversation along with the orchestration of participant involvement.

THE POWER OF DELIBERATELY UNCLEAR LANGUAGE USE

In this case, power accrues when the government takes advantage of the politeness rules that obtain when the target is talking with people who purport to be from a different culture and language/dialect group. When the persons wearing the body microphone affect a foreign accent or even speak a nonstandard variety of English, their words are frequently inexplicit and their sentences are often garbled. This causes the target to inference a great deal more than he would when speaking to a native or standard English speaker. It also causes him to tolerate inexactness, finish that person's incomplete sentences for him, and accept ambiguous utterances which may be later interpreted as representations of improper conduct. The conditions of politeness are heightened and the designated target is forced to tolerate great strangeness in behavior. That is, when standard English speakers converse with nonstandard English speakers, the latter are given certain accommodations. Since they often tend to use incomplete sentences and street language rather than the more explicit and appropriate expressions, the standard English speaker in such conversation tends to rely more on inferencing to make sense of the nonstandard English speaker's syntax, semantics, and lack of explicit referencing. The same is true, of course, for a limited English speaker, as represented in the case of Senator Williams by the presumed Arab sheik. It is only courteous and polite for a standard or native English speaker to tolerate great imprecision and error in such people's use of English. One must also note the cross-cultural implications of such conversations. If it is known or suspected that the customs of the speaker from another country are at variance with the ethics or other conventions of America, the native treats this variance with politeness and dignity rather than with scorn or malice. Such variance can be represented as the "Arab way," as Mel Weinberg pointed out in the Abscam tape of June 28, 1979.

In several cases in which surreptitious taped recordings have been used, the agents produced a nonstandard or vernacular Black English. Others, such as Joe Hauser in Brilab, spoke a kind of nonstandard street language. Even FBI agent DeVito's use of English is halting and crude, with many unfinished sentences and false starts. In such cases, the effect on the designated targets was to force them to inference meaning that was unclear from sentences which were in a dialect different from their own and frequently inexplicit and incomplete. Persons using such language are expected not to know the appropriate terms and therefore, when they use words like *deal* for *transaction,* or *buy a pardon* for *obtain a pardon,* the temptation of the target is to tolerate such usage as the best the speaker could do, even if inappropriate. Just as a physician seldom corrects the vocabulary of an inarticulate or limited English-speaking patient, so elected officials may not choose (out of politeness) to correct the street language vocabulary of undercover agents who are posing as nonstandard English speakers.

When critical decisions about the guilt or innocence of designated targets hinge on garbled syntax of the proposition made by the agent, the practice of using the culture/language difference strategy must be seriously questioned.

Even though the government agent's strategy obviously fails in the Williams and Murphy Abscam cases, as is evidenced clearly in the actual videotaped conversation, nevertheless, the damage was done. Neither the prosecution nor the jury were able to discern the failure of this strategy, largely because they lack the experience necessary to deal with language analysis.

The point of this assymetrical use of power through the use of the appearance of foreign culture or language as well as through the use of the appearance of status or class difference within a culture should be obvious. The target is forced to operate in a context of inferencing, politeness, and toleration which works exactly counter to the effort that would work on his behalf to clarify ambiguity, request clarification, and deny the appearance of wrongdoing by the agent.

CONCLUSION

It was earlier asserted that the seven types of conversational power are governed by two major factors: the hidden agenda of the government agents and the fact that the conversation is taking place for the benefit of a later audience. These factors promote the use of the seven types of power to degrees which everyday conversation does not require. It may be true that any given conversation has the potential to call on any of these seven types of conversational power but it is unlikely that it would call on all seven of them in the same conversation and it is unlikely that it would call on them with the frequency and intensity that they are used by government operatives in their efforts to thwart white collar crime.

Although this paper is about conversational power, it is clear that it is also about the *abuses* of conversational power by the government in its covert recordings. The ethical issue of covert recording is not of interest to the FBI since their stated policy is to use this technique. The ethical issue here is one of the assymetry of power caused by the use of these seven conversational strategies. Beyond ethical concerns is the question of what the intentions of the targets are when such assymetrical power strategies are employed and what the evidenciary value of such recordings might be in the determination of guilt or innocence.

REFERENCES

F.B.I. undercover operations: Report of the Subcommittee on Civil and Constitutional Rights of the Committee on the Judiciary. (1984). Washington, DC: U.S. Government Printing Office.

Green, R.W. (1981). *The sting man.* New York: Ballantine.

Shuy, R.W. (1982, March 4). Testimony before the Subcommittee on Civil and Constitutional Rights. *The Congressional Record-Senate,* pp. 1622–1627.

Chapter 5

Linguistic Manipulation, Power, and the Legal Setting

Anne Graffam Walker
Georgetown University

INTRODUCTION

Even in normal, everyday conversation, a question is hard to ignore. But in the formal process of question-asking that is central to our American adversary system of justice, to ignore a question is to risk going to jail. The power which the questioner, lawyer or judge, thus wields over the answerer is considerable, and in this chapter, I am going to examine some of the linguistic manifestations of that power as shown in a series of pre-trial fact-finding interviews known as depositions. I will be using as data my analysis of seven such depositions[1]—for which I served as the court reporter—and a review both of legal texts on the law of evidence, and in-house manuals on practical techniques for conducting trials and depositions (e.g., McCormick, 1972; Summit, 1978; Friend, 1977; Wesley, 1978; Imwinkelreid, 1980; Kelner & McGovern, 1981.) My discussion of this data will show—as these writings represent—that attorneys are aware of the essential imbalance of power that operates in any (what I call) legal adversary interview, and that they employ this power in conscious ways in an effort to influence the outcome of their cases by controlling a witness's line of testimony. The points that I will be making about this linguistic manipulation in a legal setting are as follows:

Before citing below the written works to which I make reference in the preceding text, I would like to thank Alexa McCray, Charles W. Kreidler, and Deborah Schiffrin for their generosity in acting as critical sounding boards as I wrote this chapter. To Leah Kedar, organizer of the symposium on Power through Discourse at the 81st Convention of the American Anthropological Association, where these ideas were first presented, I owe special appreciation for her encouragement and faith in my work.

[1] Each of these seven depositions involved personal injury cases, a fact which places them in the civil, as opposed to the criminal branch of the law. Together, they represent 2,562 questions, 11 hours of testimony, 7 witnesses, and 8 lawyers. Because all counsel were male, and because of the added convenience of the generic usage, I will be referring in this chapter to members of the legal profession, and witnesses in general, as "he."

1. The power which attorneys wield is connected significantly with their right to compel responsive answers.
2. This power is equated with control of the witness.
3. There are three primary methods for achieving witness control: insistence on role integrity; control of the agenda; and most importantly, selection of question type both to narrow the choice of answers, and to allow the examiner, not respondent, to phrase the evidence.
4. Unlike most language phenomena, each of these devices for manipulation of the witness operates under the conscious control of the attorney.

Since these points all take for granted the a priori assignment of power to the attorney, this discussion will begin with a brief look at the sociocultural, legal, and linguistic sources upon which that power rests.

SOURCES OF POWER

Sociocultural base of power. Whenever groups of people gather to live and work together, disputes are bound to occur. While most of these disputes are settled on an informal basis, many require their resolution to be undertaken by a more formal process, one which operates as the outgrowth of the needs and beliefs of the groups—the society—involved. As institutions for dispute resolution evolve, certain members of the society are sanctioned by the group as authorized participants whose roles, if not persons, necessarily command respect. In North American society, one of the members so authorized is that of advocate, or attorney, and insofar as he acts within his role as a representative of a recognized institution, he is accorded deference (Goffman, 1976; Philips, 1979), a cultural fact which I believe plays an important part in maintaining order in lawyer-witness exchanges in depositions.

Legal base of power. The institution which the United States has settled upon for dispute resolution is that of adversary law: two parties come together formally, usually through representation by lawyers, and present their versions of the dispute to a third party, judge or jury, to whom is given the right and obligation to hear evidence, apply appropriate laws to that evidence, and then settle the matter. As part of the legal code for this fairly culture-specific form of adjudication,[2] there are bodies of law, both statutory and case, which govern procedures for discovering what the evidence is, and for presenting it later at trial. Asking questions of the opposing side of any dispute is an essential part of any discovery process, but asking questions without having hope of a properly informative answer would be a use-

---

[2] Not all societies, of course, handle their disputes in this fashion. See, for example, Frake (1972) and Friedman and Macauley (1977, Chapter 6), for interesting examples of cultural differences in settling disputes.

less endeavor. For this reason, the Federal Rules of Civil Procedure not only grant to attorneys the right to ask, but provide for sanctions against those who refuse to answer (FRCP Rules 26, 30, 37). Thus, a societal institution, cultural norms for role assignment and deference toward those roles, and a body of laws which govern the conduct of resolution of disputes, combine to give attorneys the power to compel answers to questions properly put.

Linguistic base of power. But in addition to these sociocultural and legal bases of power from which attorneys operate, there is a third, less culture-specific base upon which adversary interviews of all types rest: the linguistic. A question is a powerful thing. Schegloff (1972) connected the force of a question to that of a summons, a particularly apt notion within the framework of the law, since witnesses can be formally summoned (subpoenaed) to appear to give testimony in a deposition. Witnesses are far more commonly called to testify by being given notice (through their counsel), but even with this less formal device, once present at a deposition, the failure to answer a question, like the failure to respond to a subpoena, can result in possible citation for contempt of court.

The power of the summons which is inherent in questions was noted also by Goody (1978, p. 23), who wrote, "The most general thing we can say about a question is that it compels, requires, may even demand a response. It is this fact which leads to questions' often carrying a strong command message"—which they do, in legal adversary interviews (LAI's). One critical difference between Goody's observation about questions in general and my observation about questions in LAI's, is that in the LAI, a *response* (blank stare, shoulder shrug, leaving the scene, asking another question) does not count as an acceptable second-pair part to a question.[3] In the LAI milieu, a question must be paired not merely with a response, but with an *answer which is responsive to the question.* Although what constitutes a responsive answer is not entirely settled, and has been addressed by both linguists and jurists alike (e.g., Hintikka, 1974; Keeton, 1954; and many others), the requirements common to all discussions seem admirably to fit Grice's (1976) four maxims for the cooperative conduct of conversation: Quantity, Quality, Relevance, and Manner. Following these maxims, a responsive answer for both linguist and lawyer is one which meets at least these four requirements: it is as informative (and only so) as is necessary, spoken in truth, relevant to the immediately preceding offering, clear, brief and orderly. A responsive answer, then, is one which responds directly and precisely to what, modifying Lang (1978), I shall term the *epistemic command function* of the question. Lang suggests that questions are epistemic requests: they ask for an answerer's relevant knowledge. I suggest that in a legal adversary interview, a question becomes more than that: it becomes an

---

[3] Sacks, Schegloff, and Jefferson (1978) note that the adjacency pair (of which Q-A is one type) is composed of both a first- and second-pair part, the appearance of the second being contingent upon the occurrence of the first.

order that the respondent's *knowledge* be displayed in an appropriate form, thus the term epistemic command.

In fact, in depositions as in trials, it is as commands to deliver information, (and sometimes to perform an act: "Can you look at this document?") that most serious utterances by lawyer to witness, whether structually questions or not, must be understood. A statement such as "Your name is John Doe and you're a civil engineer," when made by an examiner in an LAI, may not normally be met, as it might be in an ordinary exchange, with silence. Even though on the face of it no question is posed by such an utterance, when it is made in a deposition a response which confirms or denies the proposition presented is expected.

Such an expectation also attaches to another kind of utterance used both in LAI's and in everyday conversation as a part of our sociocultural traditions of politeness. This much-studied speech act, sometimes called a re-question (Sadock, 1970; Fraser, 1973; Green, 1975; Ervin-Tripp, 1976) serves the need to avoid direct confrontation with conversationalists by hiding an imperative inside the structure of a question, as in the politely put

(1)   Can I ask you the extent of your formal education?[4]

Even outside the environment of a legal adversary interview, conversants understand that such a question has little to do with either the speaker's ability to ask, or with the hearer's granting of permission to the speaker to ask. What is being sought is, of course, information about education, but the difference between ordinary conversation and LAI's is that in the former, the hearer has the option of withholding that information by answering the first part of the "request" (No, you may not ask) or by evading, or responding negatively to the second part (No, I will not tell you the extent of my formal education). In the context of an LAI, however, the force of the hidden imperative may not be ignored, and the request, however politely phrased, becomes an order.[5]

---

[4] Samples taken from my data will be identified by number as in (1). All identifying characteristics in these samples have been changed.

[5] That both participants understand what is going on in such an utterance can be explained by reference to the linguistic theory of indirect speech acts (Searle, 1975): one sentence form may be used to convey the meaning of another. If sense is to be made of an utterance, two basic assumptions must be made: that there is a reason for having said whatever was said; and that there is an underlying proposition known to, and recoverable by both conversants. Thus, an utterance such as this, which sounds and looks on paper like a request for permission to perform an act, is instead issued and understood as a request to deliver information.

The fact that the witness is not free to refuse, without penalty, to respond to questions posed in LAI's, whether phrased, 'Can I ask you...' or 'Tell me...,' supports my contention that these utterances are not requests for information, as some have suggested (e.g., Danet et al., 1976, p. 5) but are instead commands.

MEASURES OF POWER

Role integrity. Sometimes, of course, for reasons I will not go into here,[6] the witness's answer, even though informative, falls short of the additional requirement that it be responsive. When that happens, advises Morrill in a text on trial techniques (1976, p. 63): "...the examiner should immediately take measures to correct the situation. He must be in complete control at all times." Although this warning deals with cross examination during trials, "being in control" is a measure of power neither restricted to that setting, nor solely identified with the right to demand a responsive answer. Control is also associated with role integrity, which is viewed as inviolate and is closely identified with having the right to ask questions. Even in depositions, there is a unanimous insistence on refusal to share the role of questioner with the witness. On this subject, one legal author writes (Summit, 1978, p. 127):

> Witnesses occasionally will answer a question with a question. The examiner should not become involved with an explanation of the facts or of the points he is trying to make. He should explain to the witness that it is not appropriate for the examiner to answer questions during the deposition, and then re-ask, or if necessary, rephrase the question.

In the course of gathering these data, I asked each lawyer if he would allow a witness to ask him a question, and one replied shortly,

(2)   "No. I'd tell him, 'I'm not here to testify or answer your questions.'"

Another responded:

(3)   "I'd say, '*I'll* ask the questions. *You're* here to answer.' That's when you have to take control and intimidate."

And a third put it even more broadly when he declared flatly:

(4)   "A witness can't elicit a *response* from an attorney."

The use of the word "response" here, instead of the more narrow "answer," is a nice example of the degree to which maintenance of role integrity

---

[6] The narration that takes place in the adjudication process operates under rules quite different from those we employ in normal conversation, but witnesses are in general unprepared for this abrogation of what I call discourse rights, and thus frequently fail to understand why their answers are met with objections of "irrelevant, immaterial, and unresponsive." For further discussion see Walker (1982).

is perceived as a necessary ingredient of power and control in the deposition event. It is not merely that a witness may not seek answers from his examiner by asking questions of his own;[7] he may not, in this lawyer's eyes, even elicit a shrug, or raised eyebrow, or any act at all which might be interpreted as an answer. In other words, a witness is not allowed to assume the role of *initiator.* That role, one intrinsically associated with the role of questioner, belongs to the attorney, and in the legal adversary interview, is a non-transferable marker of power.

Control of the Agenda. Another aspect of power which is connected more or less tangentially with the right to ask questions is that of control of the agenda. In a deposition, the agenda is entirely within the province of the questioning attorney, even more so than in a trial. At trial, the need to keep the jury abreast of the developments in the case usually forces the examiner to maintain a fairly coherent line of questioning. It is important that the thread of the story be clearly maintained. But in a deposition, the only restriction on continuity is the ability of the questioner to remember what he has just asked, and if he can't, he always has the court reporter to turn to who can read back the question, the answer, or both. The freedom this gives him to jump without warning from topic to topic is one neither expected nor enjoyed in normal discourse, since a cooperative speaker is expected to give signals before changing conversational direction.

In the legal adversary interview, however, no such warnings of change of direction need be used, and in fact, a sudden shift of topic is another of the techniques which are consciously employed by attorneys to attempt to get what are called "damaging admissions" from a deponent. As one author put it (Summit, 1978, p. 126)

> People will not knowingly and willingly make damaging admissions. The witness must become disoriented, losing all sense of the context of the questions.

In one of the depositions I studied, the deponent, who was a defendant in a boating accident, was suspected of lying, even by his own counsel, and I had been instructed beforehand to administer a "particularly impressive oath," so as, I presume, to put the fear of God, or at least the fear of perjury, into the witness.

---

[7] Further evidence that in the LAI, questions are perceived to be epistemic commands which can be issued only by the proper role member, can be adduced from the fact that in general, innocent clarification questions from the witness such as "Are you talking about Thursday or Friday?" or requests for a repeat or rephrasing of the question are not included in this restriction. I might add here that although it is often true that what people say they do is not matched by their actions, in this case, the self-report data are reliable. In my years of court reporting, I never once heard an attorney or judge give an answer to an information question that came from a witness.

One of the issues was the deponent's state of sobriety at the time of the accident, and in the first ten minutes of the deposition, the subject of drinking had already been broached twice. The third time dealt with the morning of the accident, and the exchange began as follows:

(5) Q. Did you have anything to drink that morning?
     A. No, not that I remember. I had a glass of orange juice, I remember that; glass of milk.

So the question was asked and answered. The attorney then continued on with other topics, asking the following questions, getting one interruption midclause, but otherwise receiving short, responsive answers to each question. Except for the last exchange, the answers are omitted in order to place emphasis on the line of questioning.

(6) Q. What time did you leave the house?
     A.
     Q. Did C and S and P leave with you?
     A.
     Q. Whose car.
     A.
     Q. Was C with you?
     A.
     Q. Do you know how he——
     A.
     Q. ——got down to the bay that day?
     A.
     Q. Where did you go when you left the house?
     A.
     Q. Why did you go over there?
     A.
     Q. What time did you get there, approximately.
     A.
     Q. You were going to hook the boat up to whose car.
     A. C.D.'s jeep.
   → Q. Are you saying you had nothing to drink before going to S's, S's house, or you don't remember whether or not you had anything to drink.

This last question marks a sudden topic shift, and is one I call a reactive question: that is, it should occur, logically, only in reaction to some feature of the immediately prior answer. In this case, however, reaction was actually to an answer that had occurred some ten questions and two minutes before.

One of the purposes of such precipitous return to a previously twice asked-and-answered question is, of course, to catch the witness in a lie. Failing that (and it did fail in this case; the witness remained completely calm and cool) it serves one of the most critical functions of the deposition process: to "freeze" the witness's testimony so that he can be impeached at trial by contrary testimony either from him or from other witnesses. Control of the agenda makes such a result possible, and it is a power consciously employed in the deposition process.

Manipulation of Question Form. The most powerful weapon an attorney has in the war of words he wages with the witness is manipulation of question form, and it is a tool frequently referred to in articles and manuals on deposition and trial practice. (See references throughout this text.) The observations these writings make indicate that legal practitioners have a conscious level of awareness of sentence form and function that is missing in the average speaker of a language. Concern with form often focuses on clarity ("...use the simplest, most easily understandable term; ...always make each question as short as possible." Imwinkelreid, 1980 p. 2), and on the classification of questions as leading or non-leading. This latter classification is the subject of considerable discussion in the literature,[8] but general consensus has it that it is leading to begin questions with expressions like "Isn't it a fact that..." or to use a pre- or post-posed "didn't you" (Friend, 1977, p. 35). Non-leading questions, on the other hand, are generally held to be those beginning with a Who, What, When, Where, Why, and How (Imwinkelreid, 1980, p. 4).

The awareness in the legal manuals that each of these forms is matched by a function adaptable to specific tasks in the interview process is demonstrated in the Imwinkelreid text referred to previously on how to lay a proper evidentiary foundation. (Evidence ordinarily cannot be accepted as such without a proper foundation having first been laid for its inclusion.) Some of the author's suggestions which take note of grammatical properties include the following:

1. Use Wh questions to avoid leading.

---

[8] The use of leading questions is restricted by the Federal Rules of Evidence (Rule 611(c)) to certain kinds of examination. Use of leading questions can lead to fragmentation of testimony through objections made to them by the opposing attorney, and the legal profession has, understandably, devoted a lot of thought to what exactly it means for a question to "suggest the desired answer to the witness." Friend (1977, p. 35) comments, for example: "It is obvious that this is a rather vague test. Any question may be leading under particular circumstances, and the context of the question is often determinative." On the subject of Wh-questions, generally thought to be non-leading, he comments: "...use of interrogatives such as "who," "when," "what," "why," "where," and "how" *may* be leading, at least where the expected answer is too obvious or the proper foundation has not been laid."

2. Use imperatives for eliciting background information. "You may," he says, "command the witness to 'Please tell us where you work.'"[9]
3. Use declaratives to highlight new topics in direct examination, as in "Now I want to ask you a few questions about what happened at the hospital."
4. To maintain control over the witness, "You can make a declarative statement and add a very short sentence such as 'Isn't that true?' at the very end of your question." (Note here his equation of "sentence" with "question.")

Imwinkelried takes further note of question function when he suggests that leading questions of this last type which require a Yes or No answer, "restrict the witness's opportunity to speak" and therefore should consistently be used on cross examination. By this advice, he explicitly recognizes the first of the two measures of control I referred to earlier as inhering in choice of question type (limiting the answer). The fact that leading questions combine this capability with that of permitting the examiner to phrase the "facts" as he wishes, makes this grammatical form the quintessential tool of linguistic manipulation.

As the above excerpts show, legal practitioners recognize and utilize some relationship between linguistic form and function. Further, they assume for that relationship a basis upon which control over the evidence can be achieved via control over witness testimony. But this assumption is based only on long-standing belief and practice (Marshall et al., 1971), and except for the work of psychologists (which dates back to the early 1900's, Marshall et al., 1971, p. 1620), there has been little actual empirical investigation by any discipline into the intersection of control, language, and the law. Further, the psychological studies have predictably dealt more with effects of phenomena such as accuracy of recall in relation to question-type than with the linguistic study of the structure of the question itself, or with a match-up, statistical or otherwise, between the intended effect and the actual result of question and corresponding answer. Studies which approach these problems are only recently appearing on the scene. One such is a seminal article by Danet, Kermish, Rafn, and Stayman (1976) on the use of language to construct reality in the courtroom. In this work, which takes a linguistic approach to problems of courtroom language, the authors study questions in the light of coerciveness, that is, the power a question has to control the content of an answer. Basing their definition on a theory of speech acts, they identify a coercive question as one in which the illocutionary force (speaker intention) is unmitigated, with the examiner taking the full respon-

---

[9] Note that his wording, "command the witness" provides still more evidence for the espitemic command functions of questions in LAI's.

sibility for that force. The function of such a question is postulated to be the coercion of a desired answer: i.e., one that agrees with the proposition put forward by the questioner. One extreme example provided by my own data is the following tag question introduced by a truth clause:

(7) "As a matter of fact, when you saw Dr. D. on January 11, 1982, you reported to him that you had been working all along without any significant problems, isn't that correct?"

By asking this question, the attorney accomplished several tasks. One, by beginning the question with "As a matter of fact," he provided the expectation that the proposition that followed was true. Second, he phrased as a question a proposition which during the course of the deposition had never been put forward by the witness. And finally, he added the tag as a forceful suggestion that she accept his version of the event.

Woodbury, in a study of courtroom questions, defines controlling questions in essentially the same way as do Danet et al., identifying them as those in which the examiner imposes his own interpretation on the evidence (1982, p. 8), as in the question cited above. In discussing the more general question of how language is used as a means of control, however, her study focuses not, as did Danet's, on the answer achieved by a particular question type, but on the way those question types are used to control how the evidence is presented. This is an important distinction, marking as it does an aspect of trial strategy that is more easily controlled than is a witness's response. Certainly it gives the questioner one of his greatest sources of control in the courtroom situation: the freedom to make choices about how (even whether) to present certain facts in a light most favorable to his cause.

THE DEPOSITION VERSUS THE TRIAL

Throughout the previous discussion I have made frequent reference to questioning as it occurs in the courtroom, and have for the most part dealt with court and deposition interviews on the basis of similarities between them. But there are significant differences as well, some of which affect the use of the various linguistic devices of power. The differences that I will discuss very briefly here concern the relative position of the two events in the litigation process, the setting, the participants, the purpose, and the influence of both the procedural rules, and the personality of the questioner on the kinds of examination carried out.

The most obvious difference between court and deposition questioning is that depositions take place before a civil case goes to trial and are, by definition, part of the discovery process. "Discovery" involves finding the facts of a case, which in turn necessitates asking questions to which answers are unknown—a practice indulged in during trial only at grave peril for the examiner. Further, the questions in depositions are almost always asked of the witness (deponent) by the attorney for the other side in surroundings less formal than a courtroom,[10] most often the office of the examiner. On the average, there are a minimum of four people present: the lawyer who called the deposition, the deponent, the deponent's own counsel, and the court reporter, whose primary function is to make a verbatim record of the proceedings. If she is a notary public, she will also place the witness under oath. The critical difference in participants between trials and depositions is the absence of judge or jury, and I will return to the significance this has shortly.

The two basic purposes of the deposition, to which I have referred earlier, are (1) to secure the other side's version of the case, and (2) to "freeze" the testimony of the deponent. Kelner and McGovern (1980, pp. 5.1–5.2) explain the function and importance of the deposition as follows:

> The oral deposition is one of the most useful tools available to the trial attorney. The acquisition of a version of the facts from a witness or party prior to trial enables the practitioner to evaluate and predict a substantial portion of the actual testimony at trial...Should a witness or party alter testimony, the deposition becomes a valuable weapon for impeachment. The knowledge that prior sworn statements exist will dissuade most persons from making conscious changes in their testimony in the courtroom. The importance of depositions cannot be overstated; they should be regarded as the cornerstone of the pretrial proceedings.

Thus the primary function of the deposition is to *prepare* for trial.[11]

A further difference between trial and deposition questioning concerns the type of questioning provided for. During a trial, direct examination is that conducted by an attorney of his own witness, and it must of course precede the cross examination, which, if it occurs at all, is carried out by the other side. Generally speaking, given one witness, direct examination is the function of the "friendly" attorney and cross examination the function of the "unfriendly" one. (Cross examination of one's own witness, unless he is designated as an adverse witness, always provides the occasion for objection by the other side.) In a deposition, however, the two types of questioning

---

[10] I have court reported several depositions inside courtrooms rather than in private offices at the request of attorneys who told me they wanted to use that setting as intimidation of the witness. I have, on the other hand, also taken depositions in a park setting on a picnic table.

[11] It might be argued that if the deposition is only preparation for trial, then the strikingly asymmetric shape of power in pretrial discovery cannot be too important. But the fact is that far more civil actions are settled than ever go to trial, and the deposition, in affording valuable opportunities to the attorneys to measure the witnesses as well as the facts is crucial in the settlement process.

can be (and usually are) mixed, and Yes-No questions (YNQ) freely mingle with When-Where questions (WHQ), including the infamous Why? question which most trial manuals warn a cross-examiner against.[12] The range of questions asked in a deposition, far more so than in trial, is thus partially a function of what the law allows. It is also a function of the questioning lawyer's personality and training. Facher (1978, p. 119), under the caption "Unsound Attitude," puts it this way:

> Some examiners, long accustomed to flamboyant courtroom cross-examination, bring the same manner and mannerisms to the deposition without fully realizing that courtroom tactics differ substantially from deposition tactics. Their cross-examination is often marked by petty tests of credibility carried out in an atmosphere of open hostility and accompanied by insinuations of disbelief or expressions of incredulity. Such an attitude is usually unsound and impractical. Cross-examination designed to impress a jury should be saved for the jury.

The fact taken account of in Facher—that there is no third listening party present at a deposition—marks an important linguistic difference between depositions and trials. It is my claim that courtroom Q&A exchanges are characterized by what I call a "display function" which sets them apart from the "real" and "exam" questions that Searle (1969, p. 66) identifies. The nature of these exchanges is similar to that of any rehearsed dialogue whose function is to inform and/or persuade a third, listening party, with both questioner and answerer aware of this purpose. In deposition exchanges, the display function is absent, although technically the jury lurks in the background, since what is said in deposition, as I pointed out before, can be used to impeach the witness at trial. The same question, then, posed in these two different settings, can have quite different uses. Take, for example, the following question, which was asked during the boating accident earlier cited:

(8)   "Had you, prior to this date, gone out in your boat and splashed [the plaintiff] with the wake of your boat, and vice versa?"

This question introduced a completely new topic into the deposition: one never before broached, and one for which no foundation at all had been laid. The function of such a question on cross examination in a trial (whether or not it was objected to) would be to suggest to the jury that such a thing did indeed happen. In a deposition, however, the same question would serve a different purpose: to signal to the deponent that his testimony is not the only source of information available to the attorney, and that it would be

---

[12] "The cross-examiner," writes Morrill (1976, p. 61) "should never give a witness a chance to explain his answer by asking the question, "Why?"

useless to lie. Putting such a question, in fact, is another of the tactics attorneys have available for controlling witnesses. As one of the lawyers in this study phrased it:

(9) "*If* you want to control the witness, *tell* him something [in question form] you already know."

For that purpose, virtually any question form will do, which leads me next to a discussion of typology.

TYPOLOGY

The usual first cut made by linguists in analyzing English question types—one reflected implicitly in the distinction the law makes between leading and non-leading questions—is based ultimately on the type of answer expected. When a question calls for agreement or disagreement with its proposition (Lyons, 1977), it is commonly known as a Yes-No (YN) question. When it calls for completion of its proposition (Goody, 1978, p. 22), it is usually called a WH question. The rather elaborate typology which I have worked out for questions asked in LAI's (see Table 1 below) is also based squarely on the answer expected,[13] and accepts this bipartite division as marking the two opposing poles of question type. But in refusing, like Bolinger (1978), to consider alternative questions as YN's, and in identifying another type as combining the expectations of both YN's and WH's,[14] I end up with four, rather than two, formal categories. These classes are based on the answer attorneys expect, or desire, from their respondents in a legal setting: (1) WH's, (2) YNW's (Yes-No/What's), (3) DISJ's (disjunctives, or alternatives) and (4) YN's. In what is perhaps the most interesting aspect of this typology, I identify three functional classes which I am going to refer to as *Field, Fence* and *Corral* questions, for reasons which shortly will become clear. In the following sections, I will begin with the forms, discussing each briefly, although not in order, and will conclude with a short explanation of function.

Forms

WH Question. The WH question in my typology is characterized by the fact that it expects *only* an information answer, and no other. It is for this reason

---

[13] I hope it is obvious to the reader that answer expectations in LAI's do include the "I don't know/remember/recall" category when for strategic reasons an examiner wishes to confirm lack of knowledge of the respondent.

[14] It is obvious, of course, that no question, indeed no utterance of any kind, has in itself the capability to "expect" anything. I will therefore ask the reader's indulgence for this kind of shorthand usage.

TABLE 1. Typology of Questions Based on Type of Answer Sought

Function Class	Form Class	Example
Field	*WH: Expect only WH answer*	
	1. Imperative (IMP)	1. Give me your name.
	2. Grammatical WH (GrWH)	2. What is your name?
	3. Declarative WH (DecWH)	
	a. WH Trigger	3a. Your name is what?
	b. Hint	b. I have forgotten your name.
	4. Cooperative WH (CoopWH)	4. Will/would you tell me your name?
Fence	*YNW: WH usually expected: YN=fallback*	
	5. Auxiliary WH (AuxWH)	
	a. Formulas: KUTS	5a. Can you tell us his address?
	RUBLTS	Are you able to tell us his address?
	b. Straight	5b. Did she say what his address was?
	6. YN-Any	6. Does he have any other address?
	DISJ: YN answer not appropriate	
	7. a. Disjunctive WH	7a. Was it red, or what.
	b. ″ LIST	7b. Was it red, black, blue, white?
	c. ″ X or Y	7c. Was it red, or black.
Corral	*YN: Expect YN answer*	
	8. Grammatical YN (YN)	8. Is your home in D.C.?
	9. Declarative YN (DecYN)	9. Your home is in D.C.
	10. Tag (TAG)	
	a. Same polarity	10a. Your home is in D.C., is it?
	b. Truth tag positive	10b. Your home is in D.C., is that correct?
	c. Reversed polarity	10c. Your home is in D.C., isn't it?
	d. Truth tag negative	10d. Your home is in D.C., isn't that correct?

70

that both the Declarative Hint (Type #3b on Table 1) and what I call the Cooperative Question (#4) are included in this category. For any of these questions to be met with a Yes or No answer would be considered, at best, odd, and at worst would be taken to signal a lack of willingness on the part of the respondent to cooperate, since in an LAI, it is not enough merely to be willing; one must actually produce. Consider the effect if the following WH types were met with a bare Yes answer:

Imperative	Give me your name.	*Yes.
Grammatical WH	What is your name?	*Yes.
Declarative WH	Your name is of what origin?	*Yes.
	I have forgotten your name.	
Cooperative WH	Would/will you give me your name, please?	*Yes.

The last of these examples—the CoopWH—occasionally, but surprisingly rarely in my data, gets an answer which begins with an affirmative of some kind, like Sure, or Yeah. When that does happen, the affirmative marker of cooperation is always followed by what all participants recognize as the desired information. In form, this question type is the structural twin of the Can/Could question found in this typology within the Formulas, but that it is not in the same class is evidenced by the fact that its force is clearly *unambiguous*. In the context of the LAI, the Will/Would pair loses any appeal to the capability of the respondent to answer, with meaning restricted to willingness alone. Thus, a No answer would be heard as a clear *refusal* to obey the command to be cooperative. A No answer to any of the questions (including the Can/Could) from the Formulas group (5a), however, could be heard and defended by the respondent as *inability* to obey. Notice the difference between

Q. Would you explain to me why he never received the stock certificates?
A. No, I won't (because I don't want to).

and

Q. Could you explain to me why he never received the stock certificates?
A. No, I can't (because I don't know why).

Inability on the part of a witness to answer might be suspect, but cannot be considered to fail the test of responsiveness; unwillingness, however, can.

Within this category of WH questions, the question types are arranged in the typology in order of decreasing on-record acknowledgment of power by the examiner. Thus a question phrased as an IMP—Give me your name—is both less polite and more blatantly an exhibition of role power than is the mediated CoopQ form—Would you give me your name.

YN Questions. There can, however, be an even more blatant exhibition of power than use of the imperative: use of a restrictive YNQ to leave no option at all for a correct answer. As one attorney phrased it:

(10)   "If I want to go right to the juggler I will not even ask his name but will *tell* him: Your name is John Doe, right?"

So certain was this lawyer of the command force (imperative) of his utterance that he described as "telling" what was actually a question for which the only correct answer was "Yes." Not all YN questions are, of course, this coercive, but as a category, they have the same strict expectations as does the WH question in regard to a responsive answer. For the WHQ the expectation is information; for the YNQ, some direct form of agreement or disagreement with the question's proposition. Any deviation from this class of expected answers is subject to the objection of "Not responsive" from the adversary examiner himself, or to a quick intervention from the deponent's own counsel. Referring once again to the boating deposition, the adversary examiner asked the witness:

(11)   Q.   So had you continued on a straight course, you would have gone right through that sheet of water?
       A.   My logic, that was if I would have, if I would have turned to the right, —
            [Depondent's own counsel intervening]:
            Just answer the question.
            The Witness: Yeah, I would have gone through.

The form of this question—a Declarative YN—makes a fairly strong bid for agreement with the proposition, far stronger than the relatively neutral Grammatical YN (GrYN, #8 on the table), but still weaker than any of the TAG varieties. For this reason, it falls second in my typology in the line of commitment to power within this category. But add to the declarative what I call a negative truth tag—Isn't that true/correct/right/so—and the question becomes the most coercive form there is, according to both my informants and the literature. So obvious, in fact, is the directive toward a Yes answer that one of the lawyers in this study told me that he considers this tag—and all others—the "least effective" question type because "it's a giveaway" as to what is wanted from the witness. (Interestingly, for him, preposed tags— Is it correct that...—are "sneaky," and in his view, "sneaky" is a good way to control a witness.) The attitude of this lawyer was borne out by his practice: only 13 out of 339 of the YN questions he asked in this data were TAGS, and only one of those was a negative. Contrast this 4% with that of the attorney who would choose to "tell" someone his name: 28% of his YN questions were TAGS and another 31% were Declarative YN's, which together account for nearly 60% of all the questions he asked. Although both attorneys are well known in the legal community for their tenacity, clearly they differ in adapting question form for strategy according to their personalities and views on the use of power.

Disjunctive Questions. Perhaps the least interesting, from the standpoint of the use of power in LAI's, are the Disjunctive questions. Still, I have given these questions, elsewhere studied as Alternative questions, their own category because, strictly speaking, neither a YN, nor a WH answer is called for. Structurally, the answer seems to be expected to respond to some given in the question. Once again, the ordering of these questions in my typology is influenced by the connection between the question type and role. In question type #7a on the table (DisjWH)—Was it red, or what?—explicit permission is given in the question to the respondent to pick an information answer, although the expectation leans toward a "red" as the reply; and in my typology, the general rule is that the more choice of answer available, the looser the reins held by the questioner.

The control is still loose in type 7b, (Was it red, black, blue, white?) since a list of this type, without special intonation,[15] and particularly when the "or" is missing, implies that what Kaplan (1981, p. 129) calls a "corrective indirect response" is called for. That is, should a cooperative respondent detect an incomplete or incorrect presumption in the question, he is expected to correct it, even though the answer may not qualify technically as a "direct" answer. In terms less linguistic and more legalistic, a witness is expected, and thus sworn, to tell not only the truth, but the *whole* truth. The conflict between this necessity expressed in the oath, and the requirement established by the Federal Rules of Civil Procedure that a responsive answer be delivered by the witness provides the attorney with a manipulative tool of power, a point I will return to later.

Yes-No/What Question. The final of the four categories I have identified is the most complex in structure, the most ambiguous as to intent, and the richest in manipulative possibilities. These Yes-No/What questions clearly have the form of the standard YN type—subject-verb inversion which frequently includes an auxiliary—but contain in their strings a functor I call a WH-trigger. In my data, the presence of this trigger in the question overwhelmingly causes the answer to be of the information type, if the information is available. In other words, if the answer to the embedding question (Do you know, Can you tell us, etc.) is "Yes," it more often than not is left unsaid, with only the information appearing on the surface. Such answers are almost always accepted by the questioner as responsive, and, in fact, seem to be what is sought, since the few bare Yes answers in my data are all

---

[15] I do not take account of intonation in formulating this typology.

but once followed immediately by a short, direct Grammatical Wh question which is usually marked by the same sentence-falling intonation that accompanies Imperatives.

One example which illustrates this pattern occurred during testimony about a now-missing person:

(12) Q. Did she tell you where she was?
      A. She said she was at a dry-out center.
      Q. Did she say where?
      A. Centreville.
      Q. Did you understand what she meant by a dry-out center?
      A. Yes, I did.
      Q. What was your understanding.
      A. She was drying out from drinking.

Note here that the first two answers in the passage simply supply the information, illustrating my argument as to the essential WH nature of this class. Further evidence to support my claim comes from the fact that on other occasions,instead of a simple "No" answer to an embedding YN or Disj question, a full "I don't know" answer surfaced often enough in my data for it not to be the idiosyncracy of a single speaker. Questions phrased as diversely as "Can you explain why...", "Do you know how many...", "Do you know whether or not...", and "Do you know if X or X..." all were answered by "I don't know" (the WH information you are asking me). Thus, regardless of the hidden intentions of either participant, both examiner and respondent share the understanding, reinforced by the oath to tell the whole truth, that the purpose of the deposition is to give and gather as much relevant information on the issues as possible. The Gricean maxims which expect mutual cooperation between conversants, and which operate normally in other conversational exchanges are, in this setting, given added weight, and that accounts, I believe, for the consistent delivery of *information* in the LAI to questions that seem to ask only for a Yes or No reply.

Within this Yes-No/What class under discussion, there are two subdivisions: the AuxWH (#5 on the typology) which I have been citing and to which I will return shortly, and another new class I call the YN-Any question (#6). The most common WH-trigger in sentences of this latter kind is the word "any," especially when combined with suffixes like -body, -one, -thing, or words like "other," "further," "additional," and so on. Other triggers include the words "ever" and occasionally, "only." In my data 85% of the answers to this type of question yielded information, and that included those answers preceded *both* by "Yes" and by "No." The boating accident deposition cited before supplies two of these examples:

No + info answer:

(13) Q. Did anybody have anything harder than beer to drink?
     A. No. We were all drinking beer that night.

Yes + info

(14) Q. Did you ever talk to [him] about what you recalled about the accident?
     A. Yeah. He said he hadn't, he was sitting in the back seat, and doesn't remember, you know, what happened.

The "any" trigger also appears in the AuxWH group of questions, but redundantly so, since functors of a more explicit kind are already present. In many cases, the trigger is an embedding WH question: Can you tell us *when,* Are you able to say *why,* Do you know *who.* These three types belong to the Formula subdivision of this class (#5a) and are named for the fact that these embedding phrases are not only utilized conventionally, for the most part, but comprise what Hockett (1958) calls a macrosegment.[16] They are uttered with a single, even intonation as if, in fact, they were one word. Lawyers speak these phrases so quickly, automatically, and depending on personal style, often, that court reporters have special short forms for all of them, such as KUTS for *Can you tell us,* and RUBLTS for *Are you able to say.* The existence of the acronyms provides further evidence of the formulaic nature of this question type.

The second division of Aux WHQ's, which I call "Straight," include modal questions in the past tense with 3rd person pronouns (Did she say WH) and, more interestingly perhaps, a class of verbal, as opposed to modifier, WH triggers. In this data, this class is restricted, with one exception, to verbs of telling. Some of them, like those preceded by Can you, are simply embedded imperatives (e.g., Amplify, Describe, Give me, Start with, Tell me. . .) but others are not. The "Can you think of" type seems rather to include as part of its semantic component the unspoken command that underlies all questions: ". . .and if you do (think of, know, recall, etc.), tell me now." The same explanation also probably accounts for "Discuss" ("Did he discuss it with you?") which always asks, in this data, for information on the substance of the discussion: a WH requirement.

Performatives and Negatives. In the typology I present here, I have ignored two classes of questions which other linguists do not: performatives and negative YN questions. In the data under discussion—some 2562 ques-

---

[16] I am indebted to Charles W. Kreidler for making me aware of Hockett's terminology.

tions in naturally occurring LAI's—only 3 performatives occurred, and each was of the "I show you this document and ask you if you can identify ..." variety. While some might argue that being able to ask such a question is role-connected and thus a marker of power, I disagree. Role-connected, yes, but it is completely ritualized, and exists only for the benefit of the written record of the proceedings. Court reporters are not supposed to describe actions; they are expected in general to take down only words spoken. Therefore, to make the record complete, the attorney uses the explicit performative. As such, this question type, in this data, is of no particular sociolinguistic interest.

Exclusion of the negative YNQ is on more theoretical grounds. There is no point in singling out as significant one negative question type when negation has inconsistent effects across all types. I will reserve a full discussion of this phenomenon for another time, but will illustrate here what happens when, for instance, a neg is added to the impreative (#1):

> Give us your opinion, please.   *(Silence)
> Don't give us your opinion.   (Silence)

The effect of the added negative is to convert the epistemic command to a simple order which not only does not require, but will not *permit* a verbal response. Should the witness attempt to explain whatever previous utterance caused the attorney to issue this warning, he most likely, in my experience, would be silenced with a laconic "There is no question pending"— shorthand for "Say no more."

The Imperative, then, moves from one speech act category to another when a neg is added, but in the case of the Cooperative WH question, the category remains the same. When "Will you tell me your name," becomes "Won't you tell me your name," the effect is not to alter function, but attitude. If such a form should actually appear in either deposition or trial (and it never has in the years of my experience) it would render the utterance inappropriately deferential, although not changing, I suggest, its force as a command.

The most common phenomenon about negation in language is that it is an evaluation, tending to express failed expectation (Labov 1972). It serves this function in question types 2, 5, 6, and 9, but again with unequal force. Since a discussion of this problem would extend this chapter considerably, I will leave it for another time, except for one final observation. As an expression of defeated expectation, or surprise, this question type is in fact relied upon as a weapon by attorneys, although few of them are aware, in this case, of the reason for its potency. Several of the lawyers in my interviews reported knowing that they were using negative constructions, and Imwinkelreid (1980), in his extensive scripts for conducting examinations, purposefully begins each leading question with "Isn't it true/correct/a fact that...'' But he does so without comment on the grammatical structure itself.

In the courtroom, the negative offers a vehicle for veiled (or blatant, again depending on intonation) surprise, and can thus serve as a means by which to sway a jury. But in the deposition, the negative has a somewhat different function, being connected firmly in the minds of the lawyers I interviewed with witness control, and when I gave them a short questionnaire to fill out, every one of them chose the negatively phrased YN questions, tag or not, as the most powerful forms. Lawyers and legal texts may be as a whole inarticulate as to the grammatical reasons for language effects,[17] but lack of explicit awareness of form does not interfere with their beliefs about function, which belief I will address next.

Function

In the section on Yes-No/What questions, I stated that as a class, these forms are rich in possibilities for linguistic manipulation. It was that insight which led me to a somewhat informal division of question types which I am going to name *Field, Fence,* and *Corral.* Since litigation is not so much about truth as it is about winning and losing,[18] it requires, as this chapter has shown, continued concern with power. Power, as I have noted repeatedly, is equated with control of the witness, and one kind of control is exerted through leading the witness to the desired answer. "Control of the witness," responded one attorney to my question, "means information coming out in a form you want" (15). Thus, the reasoning would go, if you want the witness to give you new information, you ask him a WH question, giving him a *Field* in which to play. If you want to narrow his choices, you lead him to a *Corral* by giving him a YN or Disjunctive question. If, however, you want to play power games, you can sit on the *Fence,* and if the witness gives you a WH answer to a Yes-No/What question, you can fall back on the YN form and say, "Just answer the question Yes, or No. All I asked you was: Do you *remember* how fast the car was going." On the other hand, if the witness responds to the YN embedding question with an unadorned, "Yes," you can sit back, wait in silence, look quizzical, and then say, "Well? How fast *was* it going?" In either case, it is a no-win situation for the witness, and no matter which way he jumps, he's wrong. Now, that's control.

---

[17] Danet et al. (1976) makes this point nicely.

[18] This opinion may strike the reader as arbitrarily harsh, especially coming from a non-member of the legal profession. But it is an opinion expressed both in print and out by lawyers themselves. One lawyer put it this way (Marshall, 1980, p. 5): "I don't have to tell you that a lawsuit is not a disinterested investigation but a bitter adversary duel." See also Danet et al. (1976).

CONCLUSION

In this chapter, I have proposed that the following general conclusions can be drawn about linguistic manipulation, power, and the legal adversary interview.

1. Power is viewed by all parties as being role connected, and vested in the examiner, who has the right to compel responsive answers from the witness.
2. In what is essentially a linguistic event, having power means having control over the testimony.
3. Control of testimony necessitates control of the witness who gives it.
4. Control of the witness is attempted by means which include restricting the right to question, employing sudden shifts of topic, and manipulation of question form.

These conclusions flow naturally from examination of both my data and the assumptions and practices of the legal profession. But the conclusion that is potentially the most interesting to both linguist and lawyer is missing from this list: that the assumptions which underlie linguistic manipulation in the intersection of language, control, and law, are well-founded. The question which is unanswered is: Do these techniques which rise from these assumptions really work?

The Danet et al. study to which I have so often referred doesn't think so. While they found what they called a correspondence between question and answer *form* (length of the answer was one criterion of correspondence) they claim that coercive questions as a whole were surprisingly ineffective in controlling the content of the answer (1976, p. 49). This conclusion, however, is based on an extremely limited data sample: one criminal trial, one witness (the defendant), and two attorneys, one on direct, one on cross. While in linguistics, as in any science, a good many narrow findings prove to be generalizable, it is not yet clear that this one will be.[19]

The data of my own study, while comprising many more samples of many more speech styles, is also narrow, in that there are only some 2562 Q-A pairs represented in natural speech, (another 260 written as models in case books) and even that small sample is not yet fully analyzed for content correspondence. One core sample I took in connection with this study did show that only 6 out of 25 answers exactly matched the demand of the question. That is, only one WH question got a WH answer; five YN questions got a YN answer. Still, out of the total of 25 answers, only one could be counted as a complete evasion, and the rest supplied, either implicitly or explicitly,

---

[19] The study referenced was published ten years ago (at this writing) with the promise of further inquiries into twelve more trials, but as of now, I do not know if their findings have been corroborated.

the Yes and No asked for, plus giving other information, which would seem to indicate at the least a correspondence between illocutionary force and perlocutionary effect. Further, witnesses I have interviewed for other studies generally report a feeling of frustration at being denied the right to tell their stories their own way (Walker, 1982) and complain of the lack of being in control. So, if the reader will forgive a legalistic pun, the jury is still out on that question, and empirical proof to confirm or deny the long-held assumptions of the legal world is at present insufficient. It is certainly true that, as data from this and other of my studies have shown, informed witnesses, properly prepared by their own counsel, carefully educated in what is about to happen in the legal adversary interview, can negotiate effectively for their own versions of the truth.[20] But even these successful witnesses are, by virtue of being confined to the role of responders, without any real power. Although the stories they tell are their own, they have little if any choice in our system of justice over their presentation. Choice belongs to the examiner, who, because of his socially and legally sanctioned role in the deposition setting, has the right to present, characterize, limit, and otherwise direct the flow of testimony. It is in the hands of the questioner that the real power lies.

REFERENCES

Bolinger, D. (1978). Yes-no questions are not alternative questions. In H. Hiz (Ed.) (pp. 87–105). Boston: Reidel.

Danet, B., Kermish, N.C., Rafn, H.J., & Stayman, D.G. (1976). *Language and the construction of reality in the courtroom. II: Toward an ethnography of questioning.* Working Paper #5: The role of language in the legal process, NSF Grant SOC-74-23503. Unpublished manuscript.

Ervin-Tripp. S. (1976). "Is Sybil There?" The structure of some American English directives. *Language in Society, 5,* 25–66.

Facher, J.P. (1978). Taking depositions. In *The deposition. A simulation with commentary* (pp. 115–121). American Bar Association.

Federal rules of civil procedure. (1975). New York: Foundation Press.

Frake, C.O. (1972). Struck by speech: The Yakan concept of litigation. In J.J. Gumperz & D. Hymes (Eds.), *Directions in sociolinguistics* (pp. 106–129). New York: Holt, Rinehart & Winston.

Fraser, B. (1973). On accounting for illocutionary forces. In S.R. Anderson & P. Kiparsky (Eds.), *A festschrift for Morris Halle* (pp. 287–307). New York: Holt, Rinehart & Winston.

Friedman, L.M., & Macauley, S. (1977). *Law and the behavioral sciences* (2nd ed.) New York: Bobbs-Merrill.

Friend, C.E. (1977). *The law of evidence in Virginia.* Charlottesville, VA: Michie.

Goffman, E. (1976). Replies and responses. *Language in Society, 5,* 257–313.

Goody, E.N. (1978). Towards a theory of questions. In E.N. Goody (Ed.), *Questions and politeness* (pp. 17–43). New York: Cambridge University Press.

Green, G.M. (1975). How to get people to do things with words: The whimperative question.

---

[20] And, it must be admitted, cunning is sometimes an equally effective tool.

In P. Cole & J. Morgan, (Eds.), *Syntax and semantics 3: Speech acts* (pp. 107-141). New York: Academic Press.

Grice, H.P. (1976). *Logic and conversation.* William James lectures, Harvard University. Reprinted in *Syntax and Semantics 3: Speech acts,* ed. by Cole, P., and J. Morgan, (pp. 41-58), New York, Academic Press.

Hintikka, J. (1974). Questions about questions. In M.K. Munitz & P.K. Unger, (Eds.), *Semantics and philosophy,* (pp. 103-158). New York: New York University Press.

Hockett, C. (1958). *A course in modern linguistics.* New York: Macmillan.

Imwinkelreid, E.J. (1980). *Evidentiary foundations.* New York: Bobbs-Merrill.

Kaplan, S.J. (1981). Responses to inappropriate questions. In A. Joshi, B. Webber, & I. Sag (Eds.), Elements of discourse understanding (pp. 127-144). Cambridge: Cambridge University Press.

Keeton, R.E. (1954). *Trial tactics and methods.* Englewood Cliffs, NJ: Prentice-Hall.

Kelner, J. & McGovern, F.E. (1981). *Successful litigation techniques: Student edition.* New York: Mathew Bender.

Labov, W. (1972). The transformation of experience in narrative syntax. In *Language in the inner city* (pp. 354-396). Philadelphia: University of Pennsylvania Press.

Lang, R. (1978). Questions as epistemic requests. In H. Hiz (Ed.), *Questions* (pp. 301-318). Boston: Reidel.

Lyons, J. (1977). Semantics. New York: Cambridge University Press.

Marshall, J. (1980). *Law and psychology in conflict* (2d ed.). New York: Bobbs-Merrill Company.

Marshall, J., Marquis, K.H., & Oskamp, S. (1971). Effects of kind of question and atmosphere of interrogation on accuracy and completeness of testimony. *Harvard Law Review, 84,* 1620.

McCormick, C.T. (1972). *Handbook of the law of evidence* (2d ed., E.W. Cleary, Ed.). MN: West.

Morrill, A. (1976). *Trial diplomacy.* Chicago: Court Practice Institute.

Philips, S.U. (1979, July). *Syntactic variation in judges' use of language in the courtroom.* Paper presented at the International Conference on Language and Social Psychology, University of Bristol, Bristol, England.

Sacks, H., Schegloff, E.A., & Jefferson, G. (1978). A simplest systematics for the organization of turn taking for conversation. In J. Schenkein (Ed.), *Studies in the organization of conversational interaction* (pp. 7-51). New York: Academic Press.

Sadock, J.M. (1970). Whimperatives. In J.M. Sadock & A.L. Vanek (Eds.), *Studies presented to Robert B. Lees by his students* (pp. 223-237). Edmonton, Canada: Linguistic Research.

Schegloff, E. (1972). Sequencing in conversational openings. In J.J. Gumperz & D. Hymes (Eds.), *Directions in sociolinguistics* (pp. 349-380). New York: Holt, Rinehart and Winston.

Searle, J.R. (1969). *Speech acts: An essay in the philosophy of language.* New York: Oxford University Press.

Searle, J.R. (1975). Indirect speech acts. In P. Cole & J.L. Morgan (Eds.), *Syntax and semantics, 3: Speech acts* (pp. 59-82). New York: Academic Press.

Summit, S.A. (1978). *Conducting the oral deposition.* 1 Litigation No. 2, 1975. Reprinted in *The deposition: A simulation with commentary,* American Bar Association.

Walker, A.G. (1982). *Discourse rights of witnesses: Their circumscription in trial* (Sociolinguistic Working Paper No. 95). Austin, TX: Southwest Educational Development Laboratory.

Wesley, E.J. (1978). The preparation for and conduct of oral depositions of adverse and nonparty witnesses. In *The deposition: A simulation with commentary.* American Bar Association.

Woodbury, H. (1980). *The strategic use of questions in court.* Ms. To appear in *Semiotica.*

Part III

SOCIAL DIMENSIONS OF PUBLIC NEGOTIATIONS

Chapter 6

On the Use of WH Questions in American Courtroom Discourse: A Study of the Relation Between Language Form and Language Function

Susan U. Philips
University of Arizona

INTRODUCTION

One persistent theme in the cross-cultural study of language use has been the postulation and explanation of widespread patterns in the relation between language functions and the forms used to carry out those functions. Thus Ferguson (1959) argued almost 30 years ago that in societies with high and low varieties of a language, the features of form distinguishing high from low, and the functions associated with each variety were quite similar in societies and languages that were neither historically nor genetically related. Since then similar claims have been made for strong cross-cultural similarities in the relation between uses of language and the forms for accomplishing those uses for baby talk (Ferguson, 1978), politeness (Brown & Levinson, 1978), and the distinction between formal and informal interactions (Irvine, 1979).

In a less systematic fashion, some widespread patterns in the relation between function and form have also been suggested for interrogatives. Ultan (1978) has suggested that the kinds of constructions for carrying out the

This research was supported by an N.S.F. National Needs Postdoctoral Fellowship, and by a grant from the University of Arizona College of Liberal Arts. Jean Florman and Terry Reichhardt transcribed the tapes, and Anne Reynolds coded the data for question and answer forms. I would like to acknowledge the helpful suggestions of Bruce Mannheim in discussion of the issues in this paper.

general function of interrogation are limited to begin with. The existence of a set of question words, such as the Wh words in English which will be considered in this paper, is not uncommon in genetically unrelated languages. And it is not uncommon for such sets to have members of different word classes, so that some have the semantic features and fulfill the syntactic functions of noun phrases, such as *Who, What,* and *Which,* while others are characterized as adverbials such as *How, When, Why,* and *Where* (e.g., Kemp, 1977).

Goody (1978) has argued generally for the multifunctionality of interrogatives, or for the idea that a given question form can do much more than question. Oddly enough, the greatest attention to question functions has focused on the ability to direct or command others with questions. This focus began with recognition in speech act theory that the same social action, directing, could be accomplished through the use of forms other than imperatives. Ervin-Tripp (1976) documented this empirically and, following Lakoff (1975), she also documented the social organization of choice of form for directing, so that people of lower status, when directing those of higher status, are more likely to use an "indirect" form such as "Would you close the door?" rather than "Close the door", than when a person of higher or equal status directs another. This finding has been described for other cultures and languages by Rosaldo (1982) and Brown and Levinson (1978).

The approach taken by those who have focused on courtroom use of questioning has also been concerned with the expression of power relations, but in a somewhat different way. First of all, the analysis of courtroom questioning has been based on a solid data base of tape recording and transcripts of courtroom interaction that allows for better documentation (e.g.. counting) of the pattern described for the data than other studies of questioning discussed here. In part because of this, the literature on questioning in the courtroom addresses the nature of the relation between the question posed and the response that follows. In this literature, different question forms are carefully distinguished, and viewed as varying in the degree of control the questioner attempts to exert over the intended respondent. In general, Yes-No questions have been characterized as expressing the intent of greater specificity and narrowness of response than Wh Questions. Within the category of Yes-No questions, Declarative Yes-No questions, particularly those with tags, such as "You were at the bar that night, weren't you?", are perceived as more controlling or coercive than Inverted Yes-No questions because they presuppose the answer, as well as limiting it to yes or no. Both Danet (Danet, Hoffman, Hernish, Rafn, & Staymon, 1980; Danet & Bogoch 1979) and Woodbury (1984) found much higher frequencies of Declarative Yes-No Questions in cross-examination than in direct examination in American *trial* data. Cross-examination follows direct-examination, and can or *should* by rules of evidence only go over ground that was already covered in direct examination, thus much is in fact reasonably pre-supposed by the cross-examining lawyer. In addition, cross-examination emerges as defined by lawyers (and rules of evidence) functionally as calling more aggressive tactics, as one attempts to break down and undermine the witness's confided credibility.

Philips' (1984a) evidence from Arizona Changes of Plea (guilty plea) suggests that the extent to which controlling questions are asked and answered as the form of the question invites depends on the relative status of questioner and respondent. Thus, of judges' questions to criminal defendants, a far higher proportion were Yes-No rather than Wh questions than was true of judges' questions to lawyers. And in responding to such questions, defendants allowed the form of the question to dictate the form of the answer far more than lawyers, who in turn were more controlled by question form than the judges.

In this work on courtroom questioning which has just been discussed, Wh questions have been treated as if they are similar to each other, or alike, in being generally less specific and more open in the kinds of information they seek, and in eliciting answers which are less predictable in form and content than Yes-No questions. Yet even a single reading of a transcript of a court proceeding suggests that Wh questions are not so alike.

The purpose of this paper is to consider the nature of variation in the use of Wh questions in courtroom discourse. Here the use of Wh questions is compared in two different legal procedures. In the Initial Appearance, exchange of talk is primarily between the judge and the two lawyers, who cooperatively determine bail and conditions of release for people charged with crimes within the preceeding 24 hours. In this procedure the Wh word *What* predominates, there is considerable diversity in the form and meaning of questions, and respondents' answers show great variation in length and in the extent to which they copy or are responsive to the semantic and syntactic form of the question.

By contrast, the Change of Plea entails exchange of talk primarily between *judge* and *criminal defendant,* who cooperatively produce evidence that the guilty plea is knowing and voluntary and that there is a factual basis for the plea. In this procedure the Wh word *How* predominates in questioning. The bulk of questioning is highly routinized in form and content, in that the same questions are asked over and over in the exact same form from one instance of the procedure to another. Respondents' answers, particularly to questions with *How,* are short, usually one word, and very responsive, in that they give precisely the information asked for in the question.

On the basis of these findings and others reported in the earlier publications on questions (Philips, 1984a, 1984b) it is argued here that the kind of role relationships which predominate in a procedure determines the extent to which courtroom speech is routinized, controlling, and controlled as opposed to unplanned, egalitarian, and open-ended. In the procedures like Changes of Plea or Trials, where speech is exchanged predominantly *between* "insiders," or officers of the court, such as lawyer or judge who is knowledgable of the law, and "outsiders," those being processed *by* the court such as plaintiffs, defendants, and witnesses, questions by the insider will be highly routinized and controlling. The justification for the control from the point of view of members of the legal profession is their superior knowledge of the legal consequences of speech and their desire to protect those passing through the system from unwittingly damaging their own cases.

In procedures where the speech exchange is *between* insiders, as in the Initial Appearance or when two lawyers argue motions before a judge, speech is much less routinized, more creative or idiosyncratic, and much less controlling and controlled, because it is understood all are knowledgable in the law, and can take care of themselves.

If we think of the various structures in a language as resources which can be drawn upon selectively by a speaker to realize or accomplish different social ends, then different Wh words, particularly *What* and *How,* can be seen as drawn upon differentially by speakers in court, depending on the role relation between questioner and questioned, to exercise varying degrees of control over the kind of information presented in court. Here we see how *systematic differences* in the cultural knowledge relevant to the cooperative achievement of legal social action are managed through the selective use of question and answer forms.

Thus one major purpose of the paper is to describe and explain systematic differences in the nature of courtroom speech, and more particularly in the exercise of control through the use of question forms.

A second major purpose of the paper is to go beyond the issue of control in the use of Wh questions and describe the functional differentiation of Wh words so that a comparison of the relation between their function and form can be made across languages to determine the extent to which such relations are universal. Thus we will see how *What,* when compared with the other Wh forms, functions in many ways as the semantically unmarked Wh form, while the other Wh words by comparison function as marked terms. *What* shows greater functional range, enters into a greater range of kinds of syntactic constructions, and is used more frequently than the other Wh words, raising questions about the extent to which a similar semantic and functional differentiation exists among Wh words in other languages.

Thus an ultimate purpose of this paper is to provide a kind of data on the pragmatics of Wh questions in American English that creates a foundation for comparison with the pragmatics of questioning in other languages. The assumption here is that some of the same patterns *will* be found in other languages, particularly the pattern of more and less semantically marked question words being functionally differentiated in a similar manner in different languages.

The discussion to follow begins with a characterization of the two legal procedures which provided the data base for this analysis. Here the main purpose is to provide the reader with a sense of how and why speech in these two procedures differs.

This section is followed by a comparison of the use of Wh questions in each of these two procedures with emphasis on how use differs. Then *How* questions and *What* questions, and the answers to them, are examined in more detail. Within the discussion of *What* there is a special section concerned with questions in which *What* words are not fronted and with *What* questions in nonsentence constructions, in part because such constructions have been given little or no attention in the literature on English interrogatives.

Finally, the paper concludes with a general discussion of Wh words and the nature of contextual variation in courtroom use of Wh forms.

THE INITIAL APPEARANCE AND THE CHANGE OF PLEA

The data on which the analysis of questions is based comes from a study of judges' use of language carried out in the Pima County Superior Court, an Arizona State court of general jurisdiction, from July 1978 through August 1979. Data collection in this research involved observation and tape recording of legal procedures in which judges took an active verbal role, and interviews with the judges following each taping. Transcripts of the tape recordings were later made, and it is the transcripts of two criminal procedures that provide the data base that is analyzed here.

The Initial Appearance

The Initial Appearance, as its name suggests, is in Arizona the procedure in which a criminal defendant appears in court for the first time after he has been arrested, and also put in jail, if the charges are serious.

There are several purposes to this procedure, as these are layed out in Arizona criminal procedural law, and it is the judge's responsibility to make sure these legal requirements are carried out. First, the judge is supposed to make sure that the person before him really is the one whose name is associated with the charge. Second, the defendant is to be informed of the nature of the charge. Third, the judge is to establish whether the defendant can afford a lawyer, and if not, he appoints one. Fourth, the judge determines what the conditions of release will be—what amount the bail will be set for, whether the defendant can be released on his own recognizance or in the

custody of another, and what restrictions will be placed on his activities
while he is a criminal defendant. Finally, a time is scheduled for the defendant's next court appearance.

These legal concerns are usually raised in the exact order I have presented
them, except that the nature of the charge is not always conveyed to the
defendant, and when it is, it is not always early in the procedure. There is a
certain logic to this order, in that lawyers and judges like the defendant to
have a lawyer before the conditions of release are determined, so that the
County Attorney and the defendant's lawyer can each present their case for
what the conditions of release should be, and the judge can then make his
decision.

While these several legal concerns are, then, met in each instance of the
procedure—even if only to decide that they need not be addressed, as in the
case of many misdemeanors—the *way* in which each concern is realized is
quite variable. As will be evident throughout this paper, the Initial Appearance is generally less routinized than the Change of Plea. This lesser routinization can be illustrated in the determination of the defendant's true name
and identity close to the beginning of each procedure. In the Initial Appearance, a given judge varies the way in which he determines the identity of the
defendant before him:[1]

(1) Judge: Okay, thank you. (2 sec. pause) Uh, Richard Reichen-
                   stein, (4 sec. pause) Is Richard Reichenstein your true
                   name, sir?
     Defendant: Yes, sir. (2 sec. pause)
                   (6, 1, IA, p. 4)
(2) Judge: Okay. Thank you. (3 sec. pause) Uh, shur—sir, is your
                   true name Billy Joe—Heal?
     Defendant: Head.
     Judge: Head is it?
                   (6, 1, IA, p. 8)

Note the differences in the word order of examples (1) and (2), and the differences in the number of turns over or across which the same information
is at issue. Compare this variation in the Initial Appearance with the routinization of form in the following judge's determinations of the identity of
the defendants before him in the Change of Plea:

---

[1] Transcription involves the following notational devices drawn from Gail Jefferson's
work: Words in slashes / / show where one speaker's speech overlapped with another speaker's
speech, Parenthesis, ( ), if empty, show where speech on tape could not be transcribed; if there
are words inside, (John), it indicates uncertainty of the transcriber, and if there is time inside (2
second pause), it indicates a pause in the speech. Punctuation was based on the transcriber's
sense of units.

(3) Judge: Mr. Valdez, is your true name Jorge Valdez?
    Defendant: No, sir, it's Jorge S. Valdez.
              (C, 1, #2, p. 37)
(4) Judge: Ms. Miller, is your true name Elizabeth Miller?
    Defendant: Yes, it is, your Honor. (2 sec. pause)
              (D, 1, #2, p. 6)

Here, the form of the utterance of the question is exactly the same. Yet, while the Initial Appearance may vary more than the Change of Plea, there is *some* routinization of the procedure, so that a given judge may raise the same issue in close to the same utterance form with different defendants.

In the Pima County Superior Court, Initial Appearances are held every week day at the same time in the same courtroom, and on weekends at the jail, to meet the state law requiring that people arrested and charged with crimes appear in court for an Initial Appearance within twenty-four hours after arrest.

On any given day, the number of defendants to be gotten through this procedure ranged from ten to thirty. Before the judge entered, the defendants in custody would be brought in by sheriff's deputies, handcuffed to one another, and seated in the jury box, while those defendants not in custody were seated in the audience with friends and relatives of the defendants. Sheriff's deputies placed themselves around the courtroom, while lawyers and the County Attorney's clerk went to their tables, and the one or two court clerks went to their positions in seats to the judge's left. The deputy in charge of all the other deputies and their prisoners always stood right in front of the bench next to where the defendant would stand before the judge, presumably so as to protect the judge, should the defendant attempt a flying leap in his direction. A second deputy always sat in the witness' chair to the right of the judge, to handle the paperwork for the jail necessary to keep track of the defendants as they were processed.

Almost immediately after the judge entered, he would begin calling defendants up by name. Each would come before him in turn, flanked by the County Attorney on the right, and his own lawyer on the left, usually after the Public Defender had been appointed.

Most of the defendants were sequentially ordered in terms of their crimes, from most to least serious, so that the theoretically more potentially violent defendants could be gotten out of the courtroom early on. Regularly there was a "break" in the processing of defendants after those in custody had all gone through the procedure and before those not in custody had.

The atmosphere in the courtroom varied, depending on the number of defendants in custody, because this in turn determined the number of the sheriff's deputies, and the number of people in the audience. There was always a sense of heightened emotion in the room, of drama, generated by the prisoners and their families and friends, due to their uncertainty, anger, and confusion over the defendant's arrest. This emotionality increased as the number of people in the room increased, and seemed to infect the sheriff's deputies more as there were more people.

The manner of the officers of the court involved in the procedure itself— the judge, the lawyers, the deputies, and the clerks—was, in contrast, one of hurried routine. Those up front often seemed unaware of the audience, as if in a play.

Often it was difficult to tell from the audience what was going on up front. It was difficult to hear the verbal exchanges among those at the bench, and when one could hear, it was still not easy to understand. On the part of at least some of those at the bench, this opaqueness was deliberate, and due to the sense that the defendants and their families would only be further aroused by clear public display of the defendant's humilating condition. In other words, there was a tendency for those before the bench to withdraw from the intensity of the audience and the sullen shackled prisoners in the jury box, and to counter that intensity with a demeanor of calm oblivious-ness to it that was not always sincere.

Closer up, as each defendant went through the procedure, it was still far from clear what was going on, and even where the words are all there in the transcripts of the proceeding, their meaning was not always deducible.

There were several reasons for this. Theoretically, the initial part of the procedure was between the defendant and the judge, while the defendant's identity was established and the judge informed him of the nature of the charges and determined whether he was sufficiently impoverished for the appointment of a lawyer to be warranted. Then once the Public Defender was appointed, exchange of speech should have been between the judge and the two lawyers to establish the conditions of release. But in practice there was no part of the procedure in which the two sheriff's deputies and the three clerks did not become verbally involved for some defendant.

The main reason for this was that the theoretically relevant participants —that is, the judge and the lawyers—often did not have the information they needed to carry out the type of dialogue necessary to fulfill the legal re-quirements of the procedure, and the deputies and clerks often did.

(5) Judge: Well, is this the same thing?
     Clerk: No, it's two different things. It's two different charges.
     Judge: Well, maybe I had a release form on this number then.
     Clerk: No, I have the oth (2 sec. pause)...
              (6, 1, IA, p. 30)

(6) Judge: What do you want me to call 'im?
     Clerk: John Doe (2 sec. pause)
     Judge: John Doe.

Deputy: That should be uh,...
Judge: He got a name?
Deputy: ...Saul Luiz.
         (6, 1, IA, p. 3)

While certain social or legal roles in the Initial Appearance tended to be associated with particular sorts of information, it was still often not clear who knew what, in part because the defendants came to court both so soon after arrest and yet after varying numbers of hours, that the distribution of paperwork with relevant information was not predictable. Questions would be thrown out without their clearly being directed to any particular person, and answered without its being predictable who would answer.

With five or six possible interactants before the bar, the shared focus of attention constantly shifted, so that at one moment the judge might be sustaining talk with both deputies while the County Attorney scanned his files for relevant information, and at the next moment the judge would renew his involvement with both lawyers. Moreover, it was not uncommon for there to be more than one shared focus of attention sustained through talk at a given point in time, as different pairs or threes sought information from each other and the remaining parties focused *their* attention on the paper before them.

Thus, while sequential structure of the procedure described earlier provided a basic framework for talk, the need for information and the uncertainty of who had it led repeatedly to long spontaneous exchanges with the unrehearsed quality one associates with conversation. These exchanges gave the impression that important though often incomprehensible legal work was being done right there in public, and yet was obscure to that same public.

The Change of Plea

The *Change of Plea,* in contrast to the Initial Appearance, came later in the defendant's progress through a sequence of procedures that ultimately resolve his status as a criminal defendant. After the Initial Appearance, the Grand Jury usually determines whether an indictment will be handed down, and if it is, the defendant appears at his Arraignment, at which time he must plead guilty or not guilty. Almost invariably, a plea of not guilty is entered by the defendant at this time. It is usually only after this procedure that different defendants take different procedural tracks within the judicial system. The defendant who decides to go on trial on the charge will have the trial as his next procedure. If found guilty, this defendant's final procedure will be the Sentencing; if he is found innocent, the trial is his last procedure. The defendant who decides to plead guilty, usually after plea bargaining negotiations between the defendant's lawyer and the County Attorney's office, has the Change of Plea as his next procedure, followed by the Sentencing. The Change of Plea, then, is the alternative to a Trial, and is the choice of procedure for the majority of criminal defendants.

There are two main legal purposes to this procedure, both of which involve the judge's making sure there is reason to accept the defendant's plea of guilty, reason to let the defendant plead guilty. The first purpose, which is historically a more recent concern, is to make sure the defendant's plea is knowing and voluntary—i.e., to make sure the defendant realizes he is waiving his Constitutional right to a jury trial, and is fully aware of the possible consequences of pleading guilty.

This purpose can be filled in a variety of ways. All of the judges used certain tactics to meet this concern, such as informing the defendant of the particular constitutional rights he was waiving, and of the possible sentences he could receive for the particular charge against him and then checking to see if he understood. Other ways were used by some but not all judges, such as asking the defendant questions about his personal background to determine how capable he was of comprehending his plight. However, in spite of such variability, each judge always carried out the procedure the same way each time he did it, and thus this part of the procedure was highly routinized.

The second purpose of the procedure was to determine that there was a factual basis for the plea—i.e., that there *was* evidence, which if believed to be true by a jury, was sufficient to convict the defendant. While each judge also typically pursued roughly the same strategy to this end, each time he did the procedure, their strategies differed more from each other here. Thus while some judges asked the defendant questions about what he had done that constituted a crime, others got the factual basis from the defense attorney, the County Attorney, or even the Grand Jury transcript. This part of the procedure was less routinized than the previous part, not only because of such differences, but also because the questioning had to be tailored to the statutory description of each crime.

Most of the judges carried out the procedure in the sequential order of legal concerns described here, but several reversed this order.

Changes of Plea were scheduled every morning, along with Sentencings and motions of a routine nature such as motions to postpone procedures until a later date, as part of each judge's first court appearance of the day. For any given morning only a few defendants were scheduled to appear before the judge. Thus while the basic spatial arrangement of participants was the same as in the Initial Appearance, with the defendants in the jury box until called before the judge, there was usually only one sheriff's deputy, only one clerk next to the judge, and only rarely family members or friends in the audience. Here the bored calm that those before the bar in the Initial Appearance attempted to convey was real and pervasive.

In contrast to the Initial Appearance, everything that went on during the court sessions when the Changes of Plea were held was audible from any position in the courtroom, and much of it was comprehensible.

This procedure, like the beginning of the Initial Appearance, was *all* theoretically between the judge and the defendant, and it was understood that the defendant was supposed to speak for himself, rather than being spoken for. As in the Initial Appearance, the interaction sometimes could not go forward without informational assistance from those not viewed as legally central to the procedure. But in the Change of Plea, this happened much less often, and usually only involved the lawyers for each side within a single sustained focus of attention. Here too, it was always clear to whom questions were being addressed, and understood who had what information.

The greater routinization of interaction in this procedure, both in this allocation of speaking roles and in the predictability of each judge's format, was related to the position of the Change of Plea in the sequence for processing defendants through the criminal justice system. Whereas the defendant had just entered the system at the Initial Appearance, and information about him had not been pulled together and distributed through the system at that time, both of these processes had taken place by the time the defendant went through the Change of Plea, so that there was a much greater degree of shared information among parties to the interaction.

As a consequence, while the Initial Appearance gave one the sense of legal work being done before one's eyes, the Change of Plea gave one the sense that all the legal work had been done backstage, that one was experiencing the mere formality of a procedure.

The differences between the two procedures in the quality of talk are differences that sort out other procedures as well. The legally significant ideological distinction that seems to override others is a distinction between talk in court among officers of the court (characteristic of the Initial Appearance) and talk between officers of the court and outsiders such as defendants, witnesses, and jurors (characteristic of the Change of Plea). This ideological distinction is based on the notion that because officers of the court, that is, lawyers and judge (and others to a lesser extent), have knowledge of the law, particularly rules of evidence, they *know* the *legal* consequences of everything they say. Outsiders do not, and can, like children, say things that will have unforeseeable consequences. This provides the rationale for allowing relatively free, open, and spontaneous talk among officers of the court, which is incomprehenable to the outsider. Talk to outsiders in the courtroom should be controlled by the officers of the court, and should be known, planned, and rehearsed as much as possible so that no question is asked to which the answer is not already known. This talk, in contrast, is usually intelligible to the outsider.

As we will see in the next section, this ideology has important consequences for the form and use of questions in the two contrasting procedures.

THE USE OF WH QUESTIONS

The Data Base

The data base in which Wh questions were examined consisted of transcripts
of tape-recordings. Forty-two Initial Appearances were transcribed for a
total of 181 pages of transcript, with each page representing approximately
a minute of talk. Thus the Initial Appearance averaged four minutes in
length. Transcripts of 37 Changes of Pleas were examined, totalling 490
pages of transcript, averaging 13 minutes each in length.

The first obvious difference in questioning in the two procedures is that
there are far more Wh questions asked in the Initial Appearance than in the
Change of Plea. In the initial tallies of questions for the two procedures,[2]
the Initial Appearance had a total of 613 questions of all types, while the
Change of Plea showed a total of 1506 questions. This comes to an average
of 3 questions a minute in each procedure. But whereas the Wh questions in
the Change of Plea constituted roughly 9% (132/1506) of the total questions,
Wh questions are 17% (104/613) of all questions in the Initial Appearance.
While there is a Wh question every 1.7 minutes in the Initial Appearance, on
the average, one only appears every 3.7 minutes in the Change of Plea, on
the average. This means Wh questions appear more than twice as frequently
in the Initial Appearance as in the Change of Plea, in this data base.

Equally important, the type of Wh question which predominates in the
Change of Plea is different from the type of Wh question which predominates
in the Initial Appearance.

As Table 1 indicates, there are far more *What* and *How* questions in the
corpus as a whole than there are other Wh types. Together, they comprise
78% of the Wh questions, with 47% *What* and 31% *How,* followed by a
drop to *Where,* at 8% of the entire corpus.

Given this make-up of the data base, *the prevalence of What in the Initial
Appearance* (58% of all IA Wh, or 69/118) and the insignificance of *How*
(at 9% or 10/118) contrasts sharply with *the prevalence of How in the
Change of Plea* (49% or 71/144) and the lesser (though still considerable)
import of *What* (at 37% or 53/144). Thus the Initial Appearance and the
Change of Plea differ in important ways in the proportions of the different
Wh words.

Two additional differences in the kinds of Wh questions asked in the two
procedures are revealed in Table 2.

---

[2] A second coding of the data base *just* for Wh questions increased their number from 132
to 144 in the Change of Plea and from 108 to 118 in the Initial Appearance.

TABLE 1.   Types of Wh Questions in Each Procedure

Wh Q.	Change of Plea		Initial Appearance		Totals	
	n	*%*	*n*	*%*	*n*	*%*
WHAT	53/144	.37	69/118	.58	122	.47
HOW	71/144	.49	10/118	.09	81	.31
WHERE	5/144	.03	17/118	.14	22	.08
WHO	3/144	.02	12/118	.10	15	.06
WHY	3/144	.02	9/118	.08	12	.05
WHICH	6/144	.04	1/118	.01	7	.02
WHEN	3/144	.02	0/118	.00	3	.01
TOTALS	144	.99	118	1.00	262	1.00

TABLE 2.   Variation in Wh Question Form

| | FULL S | | | | NON-S | | | |
| | Wh Fronting | | No Fronting | | Wh Fronting | | No Fronting | |
	COP	IA	COP	IA	COP	IA	COP	IA
WHAT (122)	46	43	4	13	3	5	0	8
HOW (81)	69	9	0	0	2	1	0	0
WHERE (22)	5	10	0	0	0	7	0	0
WHO (15)	2	9	1	0	0	2	0	1
WHY (12)	3	8	0	0	0	1	0	0
WHICH (7)	4	1	0	0	2	0	0	0
WHEN (3)	3	0	0	0	0	0	0	0
TOTALS (262)	132	80	5	13	7	16	0	9

IA   = 118
COP = 144

First, *more Wh questions that lack a full sentence surface form, appearing alone or in phrases, occur in the Initial Appearance.* As defined here, full sentence Wh questions have a surface subject and predicate, while non-sentence Wh questions do not, although they can be interpreted as elliptic *versions* of full sentences.

(7)   Judge: Did they do that one on uh, ...
      Clerk: *What?* Yeah, they finished that one.
                  (IA, #9)

(8) Defendant: (Yeah, both).
     Judge: *Yeah, what?*
     Defendant: Both
                 (IA, #47)

(9) Defendant: Yeah.
     Judge: *What kind of a machine?* Tell me about it.
                 (COP, #75)

Thus, as Table 3 indicates, while only 5% of the Wh questions in the Change of Plea are nonsentences, 21% of the Wh questions in the Initial Appearance are in nonsentence forms. Second, the Initial Appearance also shows a higher proportion of Wh questions in which Wh-fronting does not take place, as in the following examples.

(10) Judge: At ten (2 sec. pause). *And the trial is November what?*
     Clerk: Twenty (3 sec. pause) twenty-second. Twenty-two.
                 (IA #117)

(11) Judge: ...Uh, I think it's *what*-up to one half of the/e'ex-
                 posed/time?

     County
     Attorney: /Yeh./
                 (COP #15)

(12) Clerk: Pretrial, November the 14th——
     Judge: *At what time?*
     Clerk: Two o'clock.
                 (IA #83)

Thus as Table 4 indicates, sentences in which the Wh-word is not fronted comprise 19% of the Wh question sample from the Initial Appearance, but only 3% of the Wh questions from the Change of Plea.

The bulk of both the nonsentence Wh questions and the questions without Wh fronting are *What* questions, in both procedures. Sixteen of 32, or 50% of the non-sentences are *What*. Of the Wh questions that lack fronting 25/27, 93% are also *What* questions. Thus the greater prevalence of *What*

TABLE 3.   Full Sentence and Nonsentence Wh Questions in the Change of Plea and the Initial Appearance

FULL S WH				NON-S WH			
COP		IA		COP		IA	
n	%	n	%	n	%	n	%
137/144	.95	93/118	.79	7/144	.05	25/118	.21

TABLE 4. Wh Fronting in Wh Questions

Wh-Fronting				No Wh-Fronting			
COP		IA		COP		IA	
n	%	n	%	n	%	n	%
39/144	.97	96/118	.81	5/144	.03	22/118	.19

in the Initial Appearance is related to the greater frequency of nonsentence questions and questions lacking Wh fronting in the Initial Appearance.

In order to more fully understand how the use of Wh questions differs in the two legal procedures under consideration, we will turn now to a more detailed comparison of the uses of *How* and *What* in the corpus as a whole.

HOW QUESTIONS

As I have already indicated, *How* is the second most frequent Wh word in the sample that combines both procedures, comprising 31% of all Wh questions. And it is far more common in the Change of Plea (49%) than in the Initial Apprearance (9%).

In contrast with the sample of Wh questions as a whole, and with *What* in particular, the *How* sample contains *no* instances of constructions in which *How* is not fronted, or not the first word in the question utterance. This does not mean *How* cannot or does not appear in sentences in which it is not fronted in contexts other than those discussed here. For example, one can say 'You are going *how*?' But this does not happen in this data.

There are also only three nonsentence *How* in the sample. One of these is an incomplete question:

3) Judge: OK. And ho' intoxicated—you say you were intoxicated, tell me why you say you were intoxicated.
             (COP, 12)

The second is actually a yes-no question.

4) Defense
    lawyer: Thirty days.
    Judge: *How 'bout the, uh, fourteenth of March?* That's a Wednesday.
             (COP, 39)

The third is the only one which resembles *What* questions we'll consider further on.

(15)   Defendant: I got some money.
       Defense
       lawyer: *How much?*
       Defendant: I got, uh, six hundred dollars, but it's gonna take me
                    half that to get back.
                          (IA, 59)

Thus while for the sample as a whole, 81% (212/262) of the questions are in
full sentence, Wh-fronted forms, 96% (78/81) of the *How* questions take
this form.

The *How* questions in this sample are for the most part routinized within
each procedure, and they are the kinds of questions that appear in routinized
speech in other contexts, especially bureaucratic contexts:

(16)   Defendant: Twenty-one, twenty-two.
       Judge: Uh, *How much school have you had,* sir?
       Defendant: Uh, I've got a (GED).
                          (COP, 8)

(17)   Defense
       lawyer: It's nineteen oh four and two.
       Judge: Nineteen oh four, nineteen oh two. *How do you plead
                    to, uh, both of those, uh...*
       Defendant: Guilty.
                          (COP, 138)

(18)   Defendant: Yes, sir.
       Judge: *How old are you,* sir?
       Defendant: Twenty-six.
                          (COP, 25)

When routinized questions, or questions that repeatedly appear in the same
form, are compared in the *How* sample for each procedure in Table 5, it is
evident that a large proportion of the *How* sample is devoted to routinized
questions. It is also evident that a greater proportion of the Change of Plea
sample of *How* questions is devoted to routinized questions then is the case
in the Initial Appearance.

TABLE 5.   Routinized *How* Questions

	COP		IA		Total	
	n	%	n	%	n	%
Routinized *How*	55/71	.77	4/10	.40	59/81	.73
Non-routinized *How*	16/17	.23	6/10	.60	22/81	.27

Thus *How* questions which appear in exactly the same semantic and syntactic form in each instance of the procedure comprise 77% of the *How* questions in the Change of Plea, but only 40% of the *How* questions in the Initial Appearance.

These routinized questions for the most part elicit single word responses, as in examples (17) and (18) above. Such responses are in keeping with the generally routine and routinized nature of the *How* questions. Thus when such questions are asked in nonlegal contexts, as when a child is asked how old he is, they yield one-word responses then as well.

How can occur in open questions that leave the respondent much choice as to the length and form of response,

19) Defendant: Yes, I went to—I took it to the store.
    Judge: Alright. *How did you get the prescription itself?*
    Defendant: Uhhmm—from a doctor.
    (COP, 49)

20) Judge: ... You are a-a-according to this motion for withdrawal you already represent him on the, uh, pending Pima County felony case.
    Defense
    lawyer: *How can that be, though?*
    Defendant: Ain't nobody ever represent me on uh—on that/( )/.

But such *How* questions appear infrequently in this data base, where 73% of all *How* questions are routinized. And this may well be true of *How* questions in other contexts. The high proportion of full and fronted *How* questions in the Change of Plea, their routinized nature, and the short answers given to such questions, directed overwhelmingly from judge to defendant, contribute greatly to the overall impression of the Change of Plea as rehearsed, routinized, and controlled interaction. In this data base *How* questions function more like Yes-No questions than do the other Wh questions, as we will see further.

WHAT QUESTIONS

What questions differ from *How* questions in several obvious ways in the data base at hand.

First, when compared with *How*, relatively few *What* questions are routine questions, in which the same substantive question is asked repeatedly to different defendants in the same form, though some are, as Table 6 indicates.

TABLE 6.   Routinized and Non-Routinized *What*

	COP		IA		Total	
	N	%	N	%	N	%
Routinized *What*	27/53	.51	28/69	.41	55/122	.45
Non-Routinized *What*	26/53	.49	41/69	.59	67/122	.55

There are more routinized *What* in the Change of Plea (51%) than in the Initial Appearance (41%), just as there are more routinized *How* in the Change of Plea, in keeping with the overall greater routinization of the Change of Plea as a whole. More importantly, however, a smaller proportion of the *What* questions are devoted to routinized questions in both procedures, when compared with *How* questions. Thus while 73% of all *How* questions were routinized, only 45% of all *What* questions are routinized in the data base as a whole. In the Change of Plea, most of the nonroutinized *What* questions are either asked by the judge to the defendant while he is establishing a factual basis for a plea or are asked to lawyers. In the Initial Appearance, such questions appear throughout the procedure, usually between the lawyers and the judge.

It is interesting to note that some of the routinized *What* questions cover precisely the same substantive concerns as the *How* questions in examples (16), (17), and (18).

(21) Defendant: Eighteen.
    Judge: *What years of school did you finish?* (2 sec. pause). Finish high school?
    Defendant: No.
        (COP, 29)

(22) Judge: ...Open-ended, either, uh, Class Five Felony or Class Two Misdemeanor. *What is your Plea?*
    Defendant: Guilty.
        (COP, 143)

(23) Defendant: Uh, two years of college. /( )/( ).
    Judge: /OK/. And are you—wh—*what's your age?*
    Defendant: Uh, twenty-five.
        (COP, 82)

These examples make it clear that choice of Wh form is not determined by the type of semantic meaning sought alone, because they demonstrate that the same information can be sought through more than one Wh form. They also suggest the greater functional range of *What* compared to the other Wh questions.

While the routinized *What* questions such as these generally elicit single word utterances as responses, the nonroutinized *What* questions vary considerably in their openness, in the relation of question form to answer form, and in the length of answers.

(24) Judge: ...You really don't want to plead guilty to something like that.

Defendant: *What—what am I charged with?*

Judge: Shoplifting. Carries up to six months in the County Jail and up to three hundred dollar fine.
(IA, 104)

(25) Judge: /Alright, that's enough for that one/, *what about this possession?*

Police: OK, the car was found (2 sec. pause) to be stolen, it was found in the alley two houses down from where he's been staying, his footprints were found at the——
(IA, 33)

In general, the *What* samples show a much higher proportion of long answers such as those in the above two examples than the *How* sample.

The initial impression from these differences between *How* and *What* questions is that *How* has a considerably narrower functional range than *What*. *How* appears in the same routinized questions over and over. *What* is more productive, in that it enters more into spontaneous questions that ask for idiosyncratic information, which may never be asked for again.

When the relation between syntactic form and function of *What* questions is examined, this sense of a greater functional range for *What* is furthered. As I have already suggested in the discussion of *How, What* appears more in constructions that do not have full surface sentence form and in forms in which the Wh word has not been fronted.

Thus as Table 7 indicates, 20% of *What* questions have *no* fronting, while 0 percent of *How* questions lack fronting. And, as Table 8 indicates, 13% of the *What* questions are nonsentences, while only 4% of the *How* questions are non-sentences.

TABLE 7. Fronting of Wh in *How* and *What* Questions

	Fronting					No Fronting				
	COP		IA		T	COP		IA		T
	n	%	n	%		n	%	n	%	
WHAT	49/122	.40	48/122	.39	.80	4/122	.03	21/122	.17	.20
HOW	71/81	.88	10/81	.12	1.00	0/81	.00	0/81	.00	.00

TABLE 8. Full Sentences and Non-Sentences in *WHAT* and *HOW* Questions

	Full Sentence						Nonsentences					
	COP		IA		T		COP		IA		T	
	n	%	n	%	n	%	n	%	n	%	n	%
WHAT	50/122	.41	56/122	.46	106/122	.87	3/122	.02	13/122	.11	16/122	.13
HOW	69/81	.85	9/81	.11	78/81	.96	2/81	.02	1/81	.01	3/81	.04

We will now look more closely at the questions which lack fronting and full sentence form to better understand the nature and the causes of these differences between *What* and *How* questions.

What Questions Without Wh Fronting

In discussions of American English questions, the movement of the Wh word to sentence-initial position is treated as characteristic of Wh questions, along with inversion of subject and auxiliary verb. The exception to this question form for English Wh questions that has been noted in the literature is the so-called echo question, which repeats the preceding utterance, but replaces part of it with a Wh word, as in:

A.   I have money.
B.   You have what?

While there are instances of such questions among some *nonsentence forms* in the *What* data base, no full sentence forms of this type appear. All of the instances of nonfronted *What* are, of course, object questions. And most of the instances of nonfronted full sentence Wh in this data base fall into one of two types, which will be referred to here as *planned* and *unplanned,* using the term much as Ochs (1979) has used it.

　　1. *Planned.* In the one section of the Initial Appearance where the judge informs the defendant of the times at which future legal proceedings will occur, 9 of the 18 full sentence nonfrontal *What* occur in constructions in which the judge ends a declarative form with a *What* form asking for a date or time.

(24)　Judge:　　　...We'll give you a Review Hearing—*this'll be heard September the fourteenth at what time?*
　　　Clerk:　　　Two-uh three o'clock.
　　　　　　　　　(IA 26)

(25)　Clerk:　　　Pretrial, November the fourteenth——
　　　Judge:　　　*At what time?*

Clerk: Two o'clock.
            (IA 83)

These questions ended not in a rising question tone, but rather in a low tone, like a declarative.

Note here that in both of the examples, *What* is in a prepositional phrase. Note also that while in the first example, the judge builds on his own utterance, in the second he builds on the utterance of another, yet the forms are otherwise similar. Most of the examples of questions added onto the utterances of others are in the form of prepositional phrases, which, like other units that can be moved from the end to the beginning of a sentence (e.g., Green, 1980), are often used by a next speaker to build onto the utterances of the last speaker in declarative utterances.

In this part of the procedure, the judge is the official who informs the defendant of dates, but the clerk has the relevant information, so, as if to save time and words, they jointly construct utterances that inform the defendant of his future proceedings. Whenever the judge begins a declarative utterance to inform the defendant of future proceedings, he knows he will transform the declarative into a question at the end. Such questions are *not* directed to the defendant and so can be associated with the relation between "insiders" and the assumption of a shared understanding of intent.

Such questions are recognizable from grade school as "fill in the blank" questions, as in, "And the capital of Peru is what?" or simply, "And the Capital of Peru is?"—of which there is one example in my data:

(26) Judge: And the—the possible se-sentence on a misdeameanor
                is?
     County
     attorney: Up to, um, 'l be up to one year in——
                (COP, 133)

Here too, the first speaker begins a sentence, expecting it to be completed by another.[3] All of these appear in the Initial Appearance, and all deal with the same subject matter.

2. *Unplanned.* Unplanned *What* questions that do not front the question word look like the planned examples except the information requested is not routinized, and the questions give the impression that the judge began a declarative utterance, only to transform it into a question when he realized that he could not complete it, did not have the information to do so.

---

[3] Harvey Sacks attracted attention to the joint construction of utterances of this sort in his arguments (1967) that a hearer demonstrates 'having heard' a speaker by completing the latter's utterance. Ochs, Schieffelin, and Platt (1979) characterize some such constructions as propositions across utterances.

(27) Defendant: Yes, your Honor.
      Judge: *Or, I could put you on probation for (2 sec. pause) what
                   period of time for Misdemeanor, Class Two?* (3 sec.
                   pause).
      County
      attorney: Your Honor, I don't believe that the, uh, new code ad-
                   dresses itself to that any differently than under the old
                   code (Misdemeanor).
                   (COP, 53)

(28) Clerk 2:   Shall we do a/noth/er one?
      Clerk 1:   /No/.
      Judge: For/what/?
      Clerk 1:   /Bring/him up . . .

These questions also end with a low intonation.

As the second example indicates, there are also unplanned constructions
of this sort added on to an utterance by a second speaker, as in the planned
examples. All of these occur in the Change of Plea. But their interactional
similarity to the declaratives in the Initial Appearance is striking, in that
most involve the person in control eliciting information from a second officer of the court for the benefit of the defendant, as in example (27).

There are also some nonfronted Wh among the questions that lack full
surface sentence form. Examples include:

(1)   Defendant: (Yeh, both)
      Judge: Yeh, what?
      Defendant: Both
                   (IA #47)

(2)   Clerk: November the sixteenth, nine a.m.
      Judge: Nine what?
      Clerk: A.M.
                   (IA #47)

These questions have the rising intonation at the end associated with inter-
rogations.

Unlike the other examples of *What* which lack fronting, *all* of these questions clearly involve the repair of the preceding utterance, as such processes
have been described by Schegloff, Jefferson, and Sacks (1977), Schegloff
(1979) and Garvey (1977). In each instance the person requesting the repeat
locates the *What* at the point at which loss of information begins. In other
words, he identifies the exact point after which information should be repeated.

These forms that lack Wh fronting, then, are highly specific in function. The first type signals cooperative completion of a declarative and the second type specifies the locus of repair to be made by the next speaker, also calling for completion of an utterance. In all these forms which lack fronting, the information requested is *very* specific.

Nonsentences

In addition to the nonsentences already discussed, there is a second group in which the Wh word is fronted. These are of two types. The first consists of just *What*.

29) Sheriff
deputy: What about the rest of the in-custodies?
Clerk: *What?*
Sheriff
deputy: I got two more in-custody.
         (IA 77)

30) Defendant: I guess in that purse snatching, I'm not sure.
Judge: (What?)
Defendant: I put my arm in the window and I took it.
        (COP 3)

These questions end with rising intonation.

Like the nonfronted phrases just discussed these repair the previous utterance, only in a more general and open-ended fashion than in those phrases. Thus whereas the nonfronted phrases clearly specify *repetition* of prior words, the more open *What* leaves it up to the past speaker to determine how much of his utterance to repeat, and more often suggests noncomprehension (as well as, or as a cause of, not hearing) than in phrasal requests for repair. These two examples also represent the two causes of recycling that occur in this data: not hearing (29) and not comprehending (30).

I have characterized these questions as fronted, in spite of there being no other words in relation to which *What* is fronted. This is because I view them as ellided versions of full sentence questions in which *What* is the fronted object, as in:

31) Defendant: What did you just say?
           (IA #85)

If presented in *nonfronted* form, the full sentence form would be "you just said what?", which can be confused with an echo question, and does not occur in this data. This is the only instance of a full sentence *What* question in the entire data base that asks for repair of a previous utterance, suggesting that repair is *usually* elliptical, consistent with Garvey's (1977) discussion of contingent queries.

The second type of fronted nonsentence is phrasal, and examples include:

(32) Defendant: Yeah.
     Judge: *What kind of a machine?* Tell me about it.
                  (COP 75)

(33) Defendant: ...(2 sec. pause) in college ( ).
     Judge: What college?
     Defendant: Pina (10 sec. pause)
                  (IA 44)

These questions usually begin with a high tone and end in a low tone.

These phrases are like *What* above, in that they can more readily be interpreted as ellided fronted Wh than as ellided nonfronted Wh. As the examples indicate, such questions clearly ask for an elaboration of previously presented information.

Discussion

As should be evident from the preceding discussion, the difference between the use of Wh questions to elicit new information and the use of Wh questions to repair the previous speaker's utterance is usually very clear. In this data base, repair initiated by the next speaker almost always involves the absence of Wh fronting (as in *Your what?*) and/or nonsentence forms (as in the preceding example, and *What?*). However, neither absence of fronting nor non-sentence form always conveys a request for repair.

Ultimately, our ability to distinguish between requests for new information and requests for repair depends on the context in which the question occurs, and on the intonational pattern of the sentence. Generally, syntactic forms which can ask for *either* new information or repair *differ* in intonational pattern in that there is a rising high pitch on the Wh form and on the last word in requests for repair, while there is no rising high pitch, but rather a low pitch on the last word in requests for new information, even when the last word is the Wh word. Thus, for example, *What* can either ask for repair with a rising tone, or convey to the past speaker that more elaboration with new information is requested, as in response to questions like,

Q.   *You know what?*
A.   *What?*

This analysis of the *What* data on nonsentence forms suggests that *How* questions differ from *What* questions in two significant ways. First *What* is used to repair previous utterances, while *How* is not. As already been noted, most of this repair involves nonsentence and nonfronted structures. Second, *What* appears in nonsentence forms to elicit new information, and *How* does not. While there are also more nonsentence *What* that ask for new information than nonsentence *How* (4 vs. 1), these in fact comprise a small proportion of the data.

When nonsentence forms of *What* and *How* questions are compared with those in the *other Wh categories* as in Table 9 an interesting pattern emerges.

First, just as *Who* is the only question form besides *What* to appear in this sample in full sentence nonfronted forms, so too it is the only other form to appear in questions that are neither full sentence nor fronted. In keeping with this, *Who* is also the only other form used in repair, both in Wh alone, and in nonfronted Wh phrases.

Second, for all the other Wh forms samples in which nonsentence questions appear in fronted forms, the function of those forms is elaboration.

Considering its numbers, *How* appears very little in nonsentence forms compared with the rest of the Wh questions, either to request new information or to repair. The other Wh questions which appear in any number function more like *What*, in that nonsentence forms are used to request new information, and, in the case of *Who*, to repair as well.

TABLE 9. Asking for *Repair* Versus *New Information* in **Non-Sentence Wh Questions**[4]

	Wh Front				No Front		
	Wh Alone		**Wh Phrase**		**Wh Phrase**		
	Repair	**New Info**	**Repair**	**New Info**	**Repair**	**New Info**	**Total**
WHAT	5	1	0	3	6	0	15/122
HOW	0	0	0	1	0	0	1/81
WHERE	0	5	0	0	0	0	5/22
WHO	1	1	0	0	1	0	3/15
WHY	0	0	0	0	0	0	0/12
WHICH	0	0	0	2	0	0	2/7
WHEN	0	0	0	0	0	0	0/3
TOTALS	6	7	0	6	7	0	26/262

[4] Not all these could be coded for function due to inaudible speech on the tapes, so the number is smaller than in other tables.

WH QUESTIONS SUMMARIZED

In this data base dominated by *What* and *How* questions, the *How* questions are for the most part limited in functional range. *How* appears predominantly in specific questions that are routinized within the legal procedures considered here, and routinized in other contexts as well. Associated with this limited functional range is a limited range of syntactic forms in which *How* appears, being limited to full-sentence questions with wh-fronting.

What, in contrast, fulfills a greater range of functions within the same legal procedures. *What* appears in both routinized and nonroutinized or idiosyncratic questions, and the latter are both specific and open, eliciting more longer answers than *How* questions. *What* is involved in both the elicitation of new information, and the repair of past utterances, while *How* is only used for the former purpose. This greater functional diversity is associated with diversity in form, in that *What* appears in nonsentence constructions and in constructions that lack Wh-fronting, as well as in full-sentence fronted construction.

In this data base, the remaining Wh question words are more like *What* than like *How*. This is particularly true of *Who,* in that only *Who* also appears in nonfronted constructions, and in constructions that ask for repair. Of all the Wh question words, *How* functions most like Yes-No questions in that *How* questions most often specify quite narrowly the type of information sought, and usually elicit just that information from the respondent.

It is likely that some aspects of this pattern characterize the use of Wh questions for American English in general. *What* is probably overall the most often used Wh word with the greatest functional range. *How* probably is not usually used as much in most interactions as it is in this data base, because most interactions are not as routinized as the Change of Plea is. But the bulk of *How* questions in American English usage probably do occur in routinized questions of the sort found in this data base. *Who* probably does behave more like *What* than any of the other Wh questions, and in this case the similarity is probably related to the similarity in semantic features and syntactic functions.

When *What* is compared with the other Wh words, it may be characterized as unmarked, in contrast to the markedness of the others. In Waugh's (1982) characterization of the differences in the functioning of semantic marking, she notes that marked terms occurs less frequently, and are found in a smaller number of different contexts.

What not only occurs far more frequently and in a greater number of *different* syntactic environments, it also displays a far greater *functional* range than the other Wh words—an attribute which may allow us to link semantic and sociolinguistic conceptualizations of context and use.

This marked-unmarked distinction among Wh words in English raises the possibility that the same differentiation exists among question words in other languages. In some languages other than English, interrogative words that are glossed as 'what' in English are used more frequently than the other Wh words, and enter into a greater range of types of syntactic constructions, and social functions. It would be interesting to determine whether this is a common pattern for languages with interrogative words, and whether any of the other features of *What* questioning discussed here also characterize such questions in other languages.

Such questions cannot be addressed without more empirical study of the pragmatics of questioning (Dillon, 1984, p. 17). For example, in discussions of the presence and absence of Wh fronting, most efforts to explain why a given language might have a given pattern (e.g., Greenberg, 1963; Kemp, 1977) rely heavily on the notion of focus. Fronting itself is explained as a way of focusing attention on the needed information, yet secondary patterns, such as allowing the Wh forms to appear at the end of the sentence (as in this data) are also explained in terms of that position fulfilling a focusing function. This body of data suggests that efforts to explain word order patterns in questioning across languages should involve consideration of other factors. Thus in this data, and in American English in general, the absence of fronting is strongly associated with repair. Where absence of fronting is involved in elicitation of new information, rather than repair, *the context is marked by a special interactional arrangement* in which one person is invited to complete the utterance of another person in providing routinized information. This should lead us to ask whether atypical word order in questions is associated with repair and/or highly specialized functions in questioning in *other* languages, a question which cannot be answered without examination of empirical data.

CONTEXTUAL VARIATION IN COURTROOM LANGUAGE USE

This discussion of Wh question use has important implications for our understanding of differences in the quality of interaction in the Change of Plea and the Initial Appearance. As was noted earlier, there are far more *What* questions in the Initial Appearance, and far more *How* questions in the Change of Plea. In all the ways in which *What* and *How* questions differ, so too the Change of Plea and the Initial Appearance differ. Thus there is far less routinization in the Initial Appearance, a greater diversity of things being done through the use of Wh questions, longer, less predictable answers to questions, and far more repair. There are also more requests for elaboration through non-sentence forms in the Initial Appearance.

The greater amount of repair initiation with Wh questions in the Initial Appearance (13 instances versus 1 instance in the Change of Plea) is consistent with the lesser routinization of the procedure, the lesser degree of shared information among participants, and the greater number of potential addressor-addressee relationships. All of these factors constribute to difficulty in processing information.

The greater number of questions requesting new information in nonsentence forms in the Initial Appearance (10 vs. 3) is more difficult to explain. Such nonsentence forms may appear more in speech that is less planned, and in speech that is less rather than more formal. Nonsentence constructions of other sorts appear more in the Initial Appearance than in the Change of Plea as well (Philips, 1984b), and ellipsis due to the potential to retrieve the information from outside the utterance form is held to be more common in informal speech (e.g., Labov, 1974; Akmajian, 1979) than in formal speech.

Overriding other factors that can be used to explain the differences in questioning in the two procedures, however, is the legal ideological distinction between talk among officers of the court and talk between an officer of the court and an outsider. From the point of view of members of the legal community, an outsider's ignorance of the law means he will not realize/comprehend the legal consequences of his utterances. For his own good, from lawyer's point of view, his speaking should be controlled to as great an extent as possible to prevent him from bringing harm to himself and others. For this reason, in a procedure such as the Change of Plea, which consists primarily of an officer of the court questioning an outsider, the questioning offers the outsider little response range by using *How* questions as much as possible. In contrast, in a procedure such as the Initial Appearance, in which the bulk of questioning is from one officer of the court to another, it is not necessary to be so careful, and more open inquiry may be accomplished through the use of *What* questions.

The same functional differentiation of Wh forms may also be apparent in other bureaucratic settings, so that when the employee of any bureaucracy questions someone who is processed and/or served by that bureaucracy, one would expect to find more routinized *How* questions, while when that same person questions a fellow employee, the questioning should involve more open-ended and non-routinized *What* questions. These patterns of role differentiation in questioning may in turn be specific or special cases of a more general difference between (a) questioning among those thought to share enough knowledge *for the answerer to be able to be cooperative* even in response to the most open question, contrasted with (b) questioning among those where there is such a gap or discrepancy in relevant knowledge bases that only the most narrow or common and routinized questions assure an answer that is cooperative with the intention of the questioner.

REFERENCES

Akmajian, A. (1979). Some rules of the grammar of informal style in English. In A. Akmajian, R. Demers, & M. Harnish, *Linguistics*. Cambridge: MIT Press.

Brown, P., & Levinson, S. (1978). Universals in language usage: Politeness phenomena. In E. Goody (Ed.), *Questions and politeness.* Cambridge: Cambridge University Press.

Danet, B., & Bogoch, B. (1979). Have you stopped beating your wife? Courtroom questions as weapons, cues, and punishment. Paper presented at the International Conference on Language and Social Psychology, University of Bristol, Bristol, England, July 16-20.

Danet, B., Hoffman, K., Hernish, N., Rafn, H., & Staymon, D. (1980). An ethnography of questioning. In R. Shuy & Shnukal (Eds.). *Language use and the uses of language.* Washington, DC: Georgetown University Press.

Dillon, J.T. (1984). Question and answer models. *Questioning Exchange,* No. 5, p. 17.

Ervin-Tripp, S. (1976). Is Sybil there? The structure of some American English directives. *Language in Society, 5,* 25-66.

Ferguson, C. (1959). Diglossia. *Word, 15,* 325-340.

Ferguson, C. (1978). Talking to children: A search for universals. In J. Greenberg (Ed.), *Universals of human language,* Vol. 1. Stanford: Stanford University Press.

Garvey, C. (1977). Contingent queries. In M. Lewis & L. Rosenblum (Eds.), *Interaction, conversation, and the development of language.* New York: Wiley & Sons.

Goody, E. (1978). Towards a theory of questions. In E. Goody (Ed.), *Questions and politeness..* Cambridge: Cambridge University Press.

Green, G. (1980). Some wherefores of English inversions. *Language, 56,* 3, 582-602.

Greenberg, J. (1963). Some universals of grammar with particular reference to the order of meaningful elements. In J.H. Greenberg (Ed.), *Universals of language.* Cambridge: MIT Press.

Irvine, J. (1979). Formality and informality in communicative events. *AA, 81,* 773-790.

Kemp, W. (1977). Noun phrase questions and the question of movement rules. In *Papers from the Thirteenth Regional Meeting, CLS.* Chicago: CLS, pp. 198-212.

Labov, W. (1974). *Sociolinguistic patterns.* Philadelphia: University of Pennsylvania Press.

Lakoff, R. (1975). *Language and women's place.* New York: Holt, Rinehart and Winston.

Ochs, E. (1979). Planned and unplanned discourse. In T. Givon (Ed.), *Discourse and Syntax.* New York: Academic Press.

Ochs, E., Schieffelin, B., & Platt, M. (1979). Propositions across utterances and speakers. In E. Ochs & B. Schieffelin (Eds.), *Developmental pragmatics.* New York: Academic Press.

Philips, S. (1984a). The social organization of questions and answers in American courtroom discourse, *Text, 4,* 1-3, 225-248.

Philips, S. (1984b). Contextual variation in courtroom language use: Noun phrases referring to crimes. *International Journal of the Sociology of Language, 49,* 29-50.

Rosaldo, S. (1982). The things we do with words: Ilongot speech acts and speech act theory in philosophy. *Language in Society, 11,* 2, 203-238.

Sacks, H. (1967). Lecture notes, Sociology Department, University of California, Los Angeles.

Schegloff, E. (1979). The relevance of repair to syntax for conversation. In T. Givon (Ed.), *Discourse and syntax.* New York: Academic Press.

Schegloff, E., Jefferson, G., & Sacks, H. (1977). The preference for self-correction in the organization of repair for conversation. *Language, 53,* 361-382.

Ultan, R. (1978). Some general characteristics of interrogative systems. In J. Greenberg (Ed.), *Universals of Human Language,* Vol. 4, Syntax, Stanford. Stanford University Press.

Waugh, L. (1982). Marked and unmarked—a choice between unequals in semiotic structure. *Semiotica, 38,* 299-318.

Woodbury, H. (1984). The strategic use of questions in court. *Semiotica, 48,* 197-228.

Chapter 7

Political Talk:
Thematic Analysis of a Policy Argument

Michael H. Agar
University of Maryland, College Park

As lawyers know only too well, and as political scientists continue to ignore, public policy is made of language. Whether as text or talk, discourse is central in all stages of the policy process. In this chapter, I would like to take one style of linguistic analysis—the thematic analysis of texts—and apply it to some "oral arguments" at the Interstate Commerce Commission (ICC). (See Bilmes [1981] for a similar analysis of Federal Trade Commission data).

Thematic analysis begins with a careful reading of a text to get a sense of recurrent topics which indicate high-level content areas significant for the speaker(s). The analyst selects one of the topics, goes through the text, and pulls out all topic-relevant passages. These passages are then used, together with whatever else the analyst knows, to develop knowledge that enables an outsider to comprehend them. Some parts of the knowledge so developed will be recurrently useful in understanding; these parts are the "themes." In principle, the analysis continues iteratively until the entire text is understandable in terms of the interrelated themes that eventually emerge. In practice, coverage is seldom this exhaustive, for reasons that will be discussed in the conclusion.

THE ISSUE

The ethnographic study of which this analysis is a part centers on the "owner-operator" segment of the trucking industry. Owner-operators, as the name suggests, own and operate their own trucks. Everything that can

Support by Career Award DA 00055 is gratefully acknowledged. Professor Tom Corsi of the College of Business and Management, who conducted the ICC survey referenced in the article, provided much help and advice.
Reprinted from *Policy Studies Review,* Volume 2 (1983), pp. 601–614.

be put on a truck is either "exempt" or "regulated." If an owner-operator
wants to haul exempt commodities—unprocessed agricultural products, for
example—he arranges a load with a broker, negotiates a rate, and carries it.

However, most owner-operators (all of those involved in the ICC oral
argument) carry regulated commodities. The only legal way to do so is to
work through a "carrier" who has the "operating authority" to haul them.
Since the mid 1930s the ICC has regulated which carriers can carry what
kinds of commodities over what routes. The situation is much too complicated to present in detail here, the more so because of changes in regulation
now ongoing. But for the most part, an owner-operator, if he wants to carry
regulated goods, must do so by working through a carrier who has the ICC-
delegated operating authority to do so.

The owner-operator establishes the relationship by "leasing" himself
and his truck to the carrier. He works as an independent contractor, though
his status is a controversial one as we will see shortly. The owner-operator
typically takes care of all equipment and travel costs. In general, the carrier
provides (but does not necessarily pay for) insurance when under dispatch,
state and federal permit paperwork, and, of course, the freight. In return,
the carrier takes around 25% of the revenue, leaving the owner-operator
75%, (less if he does not provide the trailer). If loads of freight are slow in
coming, an owner-operator may be allowed to "trip-lease." A trip-lease
simply means that the owner-operator is loaded to another carrier for one
trip. Usually the payment for the trip-lease comes back to the owner-operator
through the "permanent" carrier, who may take a percentage before issuing
the check.

During the second fuel shortage in the late 1970s, as most readers will
recall, owner-operators engaged in a "shutdown" to protest lack of fuel
and increasing prices. In response, the ICC set up a "fuel surcharge" program. In brief, the surcharge is a sliding percentage—around 18% at the
time of the hearings—that compensates the owner-operator for rising fuel
costs. When the freight bill is written, 18% of the total revenue is added to
the payment that the owner-operator receives.

The problem is that the surcharge was only intended as a temporary measure. Besides, the surcharge is figured on the rate, and rates for different
commodities differ. Two owner-operators running the same distance receive
different surcharges, depending on the rates for what they haul. Finally,
shippers who send and customers who receive freight hauled by owner-
operators don't like it since it raises their costs. For these and other reasons
the ICC set out five proposals for modifying or eliminating the surcharge.

The text analyzed here was the final opportunity for interested parties to
present arguments before the commissioners. The hearings were held in the
Fall of 1981 at the ICC building in Washington. They occupied most of a
working day, and involved owner-operators, carriers, shippers and customers, federal agency representatives, and a representative from the Teamsters.

While the participants also submitted written arguments, this analysis focuses only on the oral ones. The arguments were recorded and transcribed by a commercial firm, and I purchased the set which are the data for this analysis. For many kinds of linguistic work, such transcripts would be inadequate, as Shuy (1982) has noted. But for the analysis of broad content areas, they will do.

First of all, I will informally sketch the argument of the first owner-operator to testify. Following that, the thematic analysis of a particular topic will be done, using the arguments of other owner-operators or their representatives. Although brief mention will be made of other parties, the focus of this article is primarily on the owner-operators. Finally, some concluding comments will consider the analysis in terms of its utility for ethnographic work and its value for an understanding of the surcharge issue.

AN INFORMAL SKETCH

The first presentation, that of A, will be sketched in some detail. A opens by thanking the ICC for the opportunity to present his views, describes the organization he represents, and points out that his organization has been involved in other policy decisions prior to this one. This material is not described in detail here.

To begin the analysis of his argument, one first goes through the transcript and marks major shifts in content. Such shifts indicate segment boundaries. Each segment is then characterized by a brief topical summary. The segments are then taken as raw material for the construction of a model that demonstrates their overall organization. This approach, tied more explicitly to formal models of planning, is described in detail elsewhere (Agar & Hobbs, 1982).

The segment analysis shows A's argument to be organized into three major parts with a couple of loose but important ends. The repeated topic in the first part is the change of meaning of the surcharge for the owner-operator. A opens with a description of the original meaning:

We fully realize the fact that the surcharge was designed exclusively as an expedited method of compensating for dramatic and sudden increases in the cost of fuel...

If one continues to view the surcharge in this way, he argues, it is justifiable to eliminate it. But then he introduces a medical analogy by pointing out that to do so

would be comparable to the doctor who puts a bandage on the cut of an accident victim and sends him home with internal bleeding.

A then explains the analogy by describing two characteristics of the "surrounding circumstances" that justify it. First of all, he notes that all costs have gone up, not just the cost of fuel. He states that in a recent two-year period fuel costs increased 7.2% per mile, but all other costs also increased 24.5% per mile for a total increase of 31.7%. As his second explanation, A notes that at the same time rates have either stayed the same or come down.

A returns to the topic of the surcharge's change in meaning, this time shifting from a medical to a nautical metaphor. He states that it has "evolved" into the "only safe harbor," and then adds:

> The surcharge has unfortunately become the life-raft which the owner-operator must cling to for survival.

He then explains why the owner-operators need a life-raft by setting up as a straw man the traditional supply/demand argument that if the rates are low then there must be little demand for the service. A argues that this does not apply, since owner-operators neither control the rates nor have any "bargaining power or influence" with those who do, namely the regulated carriers.

Then he again raises the issue of the change in meaning of the surcharge.

> Although this proceeding was called to address the surcharge problem what we are really are talking about is compensation.

He repeats the medical analogy, and notes that with provisions for adequate compensation neither the surcharge nor the current hearings would have been necessary.

The next major part is organized around A's comments on the various ICC proposals under consideration. He states that most of them rely on the "good faith" of the carriers and on their commitment to increase rates. He says:

> Considering current conditions and past practices, this would be naive to say the least, and in my opinion would be like sending the fox to guard the chickens.

He explains the analogy with three arguments: the first, that carriers trust each other even less than owner-operators trust them; the second, that there were problems with the surcharge requiring ICC intervention when it was first introduced; the third, that the provision for the carriers to replace the surcharge with rate increases is already in place, but they have not done it.

With that A finishes the second major part and then makes two points that stand alone, though they are obviously related to his overall argument. In the first, he notes that some think the owner-operators are making "windfall profits" because of the surcharge, which he dismisses as ridiculous. In the second, he states that owner-operators play a unique role in the "nation's transportation system" and that they are therefore deserving of attention.

The final part begins with A's three recommendations. The first is to tie changes in the surcharge to general changes in the economy. The second is to open up a new market for the owner-operators, namely the private carriers (companies that only haul their own products).

We believe the addition of this alternative market would cause the regulated carriers who have traditionally taken the owner operator for granted and in most cases demonstrated a complete disregard for his profitability, to take a serious look at the relationship which has evolved between them and the owner-operators over the years.

Finally A makes his third recommendation, that a system be established which requires owner-operator expenses to be considered when carriers set rates. He then goes on to describe an example of such a system and how it might operate. A closes his presentation with a repetition of the medical analogy and a reminder of the "special circumstances" of the current owner-operator situation.

We now have a sense of the overall organization of A's presentation. From an ethnographic point of view, we are primarily interested in the high-level patterns of content. However, rather than trying to account for every shred of content, we focus on those areas that signal differences between an owner-operator's world and our own. Less attention is paid to A's use of medical and nautical analogies, which we understand very well, and more to issues around concepts like "surcharge," "rates," and "carriers" which are alien. Further, content areas are chosen which look like promising candidates for "themes" that will prove useful in understanding other expressions of owner-operator life.

These three criteria help clarify an ethnographic approach to language—a concern with high-level content that signals differences between worlds and that looks like a theme with potential for broad application. In A's presentation, there is one striking content area that in fact organizes the second major part—his view of the carriers. Further, though this topic dominates one part, it also serves as a resource throughout. Having chosen this topical area, we now want to begin to construct a more detailed sense of "carriers." Now we return to the full text and examine other owner-operator statements about carriers.

THEMATIC ANALYSIS

The first problem in thematic analysis is the lifting of statements out of context. In the informal discussion of A's argument, we saw how statements entered into various portions of the argument as a whole. Now we just lift statements out of other sections of the transcript without regard for their context. They play different roles in the argument—introductions, asides, background, response to a question—as well as in the logical texture of the presentation—elaborations, explanations, and so on. However, the working assumption is that there will be a pattern in statements about carriers that transcends the roles they play in specific discourse contexts.

The second problem is in locating the patterns. In some cases statements are easily grouped together because their overall content is so similar. More typical will be patterns requiring many inferences on the part of the analyst. However, one advantage of the analysis is that some statements are on display and the inferences are made explicit in the discussions of the groupings.

In the data summarized here in Table 1, each statement is numbered sequentially for reference. At the beginning of each, a letter indicates the speaker, running from "B" through "I" to cover the eight additional owner-operator representatives. Following the letter are numbers indicating the page and line numbers in the original commercially-prepared transcript. Most of the owner-operators testified early in the proceedings, though a couple of them were given their time later. Due to space limitations, Table 1 presents only one example statement for each group of statements originally used in the analysis. As we discuss the themes below, they will be given an abbreviated name in upper-case letters for later use in Figure 1.

The first group of statements illustrate the theme that carriers are generally greedy and untrustworthy. We'll call this the GREEDY CARRIER theme. Statements reflected the theme in three major ways. First of all, number 1 in Table 1 exemplifies talk about greed, while number 2 explicitly mentions trust. Number 3 deals with greed and trust by inference, since it describes regulations that should be established or enforced to protect owner-operators from carriers. This group of statements is difficult to sort independently; some, in fact, are by inference about trust, greed, and the need to regulate all at the same time. The problems in differentiating them is the reason they were grouped together.

The first theme, then, is constructed as the attribution of greed to carriers, which in turn implies that they can't be trusted, which in turn implies that their relations with owner-operators must be regulated. The greediness and untrustworthiness of carriers is based on experience. It is supported by the next theme, which responds to the issue of the moment—the fuel surcharge—and shows that carriers have used it improperly to increase their own revenues. (See number 4 in Table 1). This IGNORE REG theme—that carriers have violated surcharge rules—points to a fundamental contradiction in the owner-operators' argument to which we will return; from the first theme we see that carriers must be regulated to protect owner-operators; from the second we see that carriers violate regulations. In one statement an owner-operator even argues that regulations are impossible to enforce at any rate.

TABLE 1. Statements Exemplifying Themes Discussed in the Text

1. H80:24-81:1 I do not want the companies to get one piece of that (surcharge) because they will steal it, frankly.

2. D30:19-23 He (owner-operator) doesn't trust the government; he doesn't trust the carriers. He has been burned so many times, he has been through so much, that it isn't a question of paranoia. These are justifiable fears. He has been down this road for 20 years.

3. B18:16-19 ...something as elemental and important to us as a mandatory contract of haul languishes at the hands of those who claim they act ethically, but will not sign a simple contract to prove it.

4. G41:10-17 It is also rather ironic that the same carriers who are in this room today to remove the surcharge and who have been violating this federal program are still getting away with it because of either indifference or lack of action by the Interstate Commerce Commission. There are representatives of large carriers present today who will be submitting testimony to abolish a program that they have never adhered to in the first place.

5. E34:23-25 But as is always the case, the owner-operator has no input to the carrier's action in these matters (rate setting).

6. C24:18-25:1 For one thing, we do not have enough leverage to negotiate with carriers. Also, it is not practical for carriers with large fleets to negotiate on a group basis because of the difficulty of assembling all the concerned parties at one time. And to negotiate with other than all of them at one time could prove inequitable to some parties. As you know, it is in violation of the law for us to negotiate as a group on money matters.

7. F36:8-13 As far as renegotiating—excuse me—requiring carriers to renegotiate the lease, it did not work before and it can't work now, for without a say in our lease the only thing we had to do was either sign it or not work.

8. I177:24-178:7 As a mileage-compensated owner-operator and an independent businessman, I have no leverage to go to the carrier and ask for an increase when my costs increase on the road. By virtue of the fact that we are independent businessmen, as an association or a group of people gathered together in a common interest to achieve better rates for ourselves, we cannot go to the carrier. We can go as an individual, and as an individual we are asked or told that if we can do any better somewhere else, to go there.

9. C25:9-12 A mileage-based compensation also provides an opportunity for fraud against shippers and inadequate compensation for truckers by manipulation of basic averages.

10. E34:20-23 Many games can and have been in the past played with rate adjustments by carriers using owner-operators. Every rate reduction greatly affects the fiscal stability of the owner-operator, but has a very small fiscal impact on the carrier.

11. B15:4-6 (ICC should undertake a study) with an eye toward enacting regulations which would mandate that carriers take owner-operators' cost of operations into account in the rate-making process.

12. I178:17-19 I think that if the carriers were set at a standard by which we could all justifiably live economically, we wouldn't have had the surcharge today.

But given that carriers are greedy—by assertion and past example—and given that that implies that they can't be trusted, why does it follow that they must be regulated? The answer lies in the third NO LEVERAGE theme; owner-operators have no bargaining power. To understand this, some more background knowledge on trucking is necessary. "Rates," the price charged for hauling freight, are in theory regulated by the ICC. There are a bewildering variety of them. Some are set by regional rate bureaus—so-called "collective rate-making." The trucking industry was exempted from anti-trust laws so that this could occur. But the kinds of carriers that owner-operators lease to have increasingly been doing "independent actions," where they file their own rate outside of the rate bureaus. Because of this, and because of the easier entry of carriers since the Motor Carrier Act of 1980, rates have changed rapidly, usually in a downward direction.

So, first of all, it is the carriers who set the rates; owner-operators have to accept them, whatever they are. Then, under the new Motor Carrier Act, some flexibility has been allowed the carriers in adjusting their rates. In the current recession many rates are being cut. The owner-operators, who usually carry the lower-rate "truckload quantity" freight anyway, must absorb around 75% of the cut by the provisions of the usual lease if they have their own trailer, as outlined earlier in this article.

The second important piece of background knowledge lies in the current controversy over the status of leased owner-operators. They are usually regarded as "independent contractors." Therefore, by the anti-trust laws it is not legal for them to collectively set prices through negotiation with a carrier. However, there is some debate ongoing at the federal level where some want to regard the leased owner-operators as "employees." Again, the issue is too complicated to develop fully here, but for now the important point is that as independent contractors they cannot collectively negotiate with carriers without violating anti-trust laws.

Returning to the NO LEVERAGE theme, we see lack of control over rates exemplified in number 5. General comments about a lack of leverage with carriers occur in number 6, and an example of a more specific statement is shown in number 7—the only thing an owner-operator can do to protest rates is to refuse to take the freight. Problems with the antitrust law are mentioned in number 8, and the practical problems of getting all the owner-operators together in one place is also stated.

Summarizing this theme, then, we see a lack of bargaining power explained by carrier control of rates and the antitrust laws. The consequences of this situation are represented in the next OPERATING COSTS theme—carriers take owner-operator operating costs if they control the method of paying the surcharge and figure out a way to keep some of it for themselves. Owner-operators are responsible for their own wages, the expenses of maintaining their equipment, their travel costs, usually their permit costs, and so on. Therefore, since most of the ICC proposals to change the fuel surcharge involve leaving control in the hands of the carriers, we see in number 9 criticism because of the potential loss of operating costs. Another statement not listed in Table 1 argues for a new market for owner-operators (leasing to private carriers) using similar reasoning. Number 10 makes explicit the link between carrier control of rates and owner-operator profits. Although these statements are clearly linked to other themes, they are included here because one ICC proposal suggested "folding in" the surcharge into the rate with the understanding that rates will be raised enough to guarantee owner-operator profitability. As we have already seen, other themes show that the argument is that the carriers will not be concerned with owner-operator profits.

The argument leads to a proposal to the ICC that they control the relationship between rate-setting by the carriers and the operating costs of owner-operators, as exemplified by number 11 in Table 1. We'll call this the ADEQUATE COMPENSATION theme. The final group of statements express a counterfactual theme (number 12 in Table 1)—if the current situation didn't exist, where the current situation is in part summarized in the themes already analyzed, the problem of the surcharge would disappear. Though only stated by three individuals, this METATHEME, or theme about the other themes, is an important one because of the fundamental contradiction in the owner-operator argument that will be brought out in the next section.

As noted throughout the discussion, the distinct themes that were set out overlap to some extent, and some of the excerpts could fit under more than one category. This characteristic of the data motivates the traditional holistic assumption of ethnography; namely that as we build knowledge structures to understand small pieces of data, we will eventually be able to link them up to show their interrelationships. Until now, the analysis has been anchored in broad ranges of content in the transcript and some inferences made by the analyst. Now I would like to suggest a knowledge structure that ties the various themes together.

THE FRAME

A diagram of this general knowledge structure, or "frame," is shown in Figure 1. The organizational core of the frame is the necessity of regulating the carrier-owner-operator relationship. This general core is specified more precisely by the ADEQUATE COMPENSATION theme, otherwise one can not operate profitably, as shown in the OPERATING COSTS theme, because carriers will take as much as they can get away with, as expressed in the GREEDY CARRIER theme. This theme also explains why regulation is necessary, as does the NO LEVERAGE theme that shows how owner-opera-

FIGURE 1. Frame Organization of the Themes

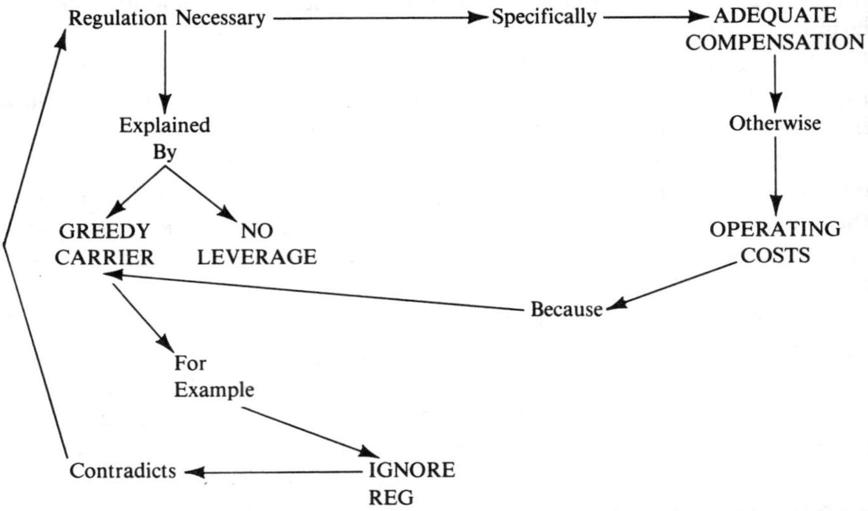

Note: METATHEME comments on the entire frame.

tors don't set rates and can't negotiate as a group with those who do. The IGNORE REG theme—the examples of past carrier violations of the surcharge—EXEMPLIFIES carrier greed and untrustworthiness. Unfortunately, it also CONTRADICTS the core of the frame, the necessity for regulation in the first place, because it suggests that carriers do what they please and that the ICC doesn't adequately enforce the regulations. The METATHEME—that with a more reasonable carrier-owner-operator relationship none of this would be necessary—is a comment on the frame as a whole.

The logic of the frame is a reasonable way to organize the different themes, but its constituent parts consist of different kinds of things. First of all, its organizational core ties it to the situation-at-hand, the presentation of arguments to the ICC on the fuel surcharge issue. Second, it contains a number of facts about the trucking industry and the owner-operator role within it. Third, it contains some assertions based on experiences that owner-operators have had with carriers. Finally, it contains some folk theories, most prominently a traditional American one that the little guy is vulnerable in the face of large companies because they are primarily interested in making a profit with no consideration for his situation.

The frame is tied to the issue, but its pieces are not necessarily. In principle, the frame could be checked to see if it helps an outsider understand ANY owner-operator discussion of regulations intended to cover ANY aspect of the owner-operator-carrier relationship. Some suggestion for this can be found, for example, in statements where additional regulatory issues are explicitly mentioned—leasing, detention, skimming and so on.

From an adversary point of view, one might want to question whether or not the themes in the frame are "true." Perhaps the owner-operators are constructing an argument to advocate a position, but the components of the argument are not based on how the world "is." First of all, the facts about the trucking industry are true; everyone involved in the hearing knows what they are. Second, the folk theory mentioned above is probably one with which all the participants in this particular hearing would agree. The vulnerable part of the frame are those themes that rest on the reported experiences of owner-operators.

Interestingly enough, this third area is the one that some of the carrier representatives responded to in their testimony, noting that not all carriers are bad, that some carriers are concerned with the welfare of their owner-operators, that some carriers have low turnover rates among their owner-operators, and so on. Further, in the interview and observational data that I have collected, it is clear that owner-operators themselves recognize that there are good and bad carriers, and sometimes an owner-operator stays leased to one carrier for a period of several years. However, given that high owner-operator turnover is normal (Maister, 1980; ICC, 1978; 1979), and given my data, the GREEDY CARRIER theme is true in a statistical sense, even if exaggerated for the purposes of the ICC hearings. Beyond that I simply don't have the data to make a more accurate statement. Even without the experiential themes related to carriers, though, the frame represents a strong argument with just the facts about the industry and the folk theory.

The contradiction in the frame introduces what I am coming to appreciate as a fundamental one that runs across several aspects of the owner-operator's working world. The contradiction lies in the incompatibility of the traditional American belief in the value of free enterprise and the controlled nature of most markets prior to any small businessperson's entry into it. The problem for the owner-operator as small businessman is that he participates in a market controlled by the carriers. As an American small businessman he articulates the free enterprise ideology. At the same time, he needs protection from carriers. They have control of the rates; they control access to the freight; they have more influence at the ICC; they have powerful lobbies in Washington; and so on. The current pressure on carriers, who are undergoing their own severe recession-induced squeeze on profitability, is an even greater incentive for them to increase their revenue at the expense of leased owner-operators.

But the contradiction doesn't end there. First, an owner-operator is committed to the ideology of free enterprise but needs regulations to protect his profitability. Then the regulations must be framed and enforced by the ICC, but the carriers can usually ignore them, since with limited agency resources they usually can't be enforced anyway, more so at the present with the ongoing severe budget cuts. The only legal alternative for an owner-operator is to enter into litigation he can not afford using time he does not have in a case that he most probably will not win.

This simple discussion may seem far afield of thematic analysis, but it arose from the contradiction that emerged from it. Further, it shows that the owner-operators are not uniquely inconsistent individuals; instead, they appear as one embodiment of a much more pervasive, contemporary American contradiction between free enterprise ideology and the prevalence of limited-access markets, a contradiction that is often described as organizing much of our history.

CONCLUSION

Even though this analysis of the transcript deals with language in a general and informal way, coverage has still been limited. As a rough guide, the owner-operator arguments cover about 51 pages of the total 180 pages of transcript. Of this 51 pages, roughly ten pages of material went into the analysis, though this is an underestimate because a few passages—one of them quite lengthy—were summarized in parentheses. At first glance, this illustrates an ethnographic paradox—the more attention paid to detail, the less the coverage that is possible. We didn't even get to the rest of the owner-operator transcripts, which would have suggested additional themes and additional relationships among them.

But the narrow focus becomes less of a problem when the analysis is put into broader context. To modify Messerschmidt's (1981) term, this article exemplifies the "linguistic anthropology of issues." The narrow focus takes on significance because of its link to the issue of relations between owner-operators and carriers. You only have to talk to a few owner-operators or read some of their trade journals to realize that this issue is significant for them, and similar brief encounters with other industry or regulatory agency representatives will teach you that it is equally central in their worlds.

The analysis also takes on ethnographic significance, because it serves as an occasion for the organization of the wide-ranging knowledge that comes from participant observation and theoretical interest. Constructing and interpreting the themes allows one first of all to pull together scattered knowledge from readings, interviews, and participant observation in a way that was both motivated and constrained by the text at hand. It also allows a connection of the analysis with issues of the broader political and economic context in which the owner-operator group participates.

Unfortunately, there is no way to know what sort of themes the ICC commissioners heard and how their hearing of them entered into the final decision, since their deliberations occurred in closed sessions. However, final revisions for this chapter were done one year after the oral arguments, so informally we can evaluate the frame against what has happened in that one-year period.

The ICC announced that the surcharge would be abolished and replaced with a mileage-based compensation to owner-operators. The figure would vary with the cost of fuel, and it would be issued for any miles—loaded or empty—that the owner-operator ran under carrier dispatch. There were some court fights and fine-tuning of the interpretation, but the details need not be described here. For our purposes, the point is that the frame in Figure 1 should still apply to owner-operator presentations concerning the mileage-based compensation. The change in policy did respond to their thematic emphasis on the need for some compensation to insure their survival. But by the logic of the frame little changed, since carriers still control the payment and nothing was done to insure adequate compensation. We would expect the same sort of arguments to be applicable to the new situation.

In fact, at a meeting of an independent trucker's organization that I attended shortly after the new mileage compensation was implemented, that is exactly what happened. Owner-operators reported a variety of carrier interpretations of the new compensation program, where many of them were tinkered with to the carriers' advantage. As an example story, let me quote a passage from a transcript of an interview with an owner-operator about his career in trucking:

> and uh what finally got me disgusted was uh we were hauling say a set of chassis from Baltimore to Jersey, and they were paying 200 dollars, they'd pay 200 dollars, we were on a flat rate, but they still broke it down with the surcharge, it was 250 plus the surcharge which come up to about 72 dollars, which apparently they were charging 200 up and 36 dollar surcharge, I think it was 18 percent then, ok, and then the same thing coming back on the other end, but they gave us-so that gave them 400 yeah right, we got uh 250 plus the surcharge which was 72 dollars, they lost the freight from this one outfit due to a billing error, these people were uh ABC lines, they're particular about billing, and XYZ's office somehow made a mistake and they lost them as a customer, so over a period of time they were trying to get them back, so what they did they cut rate again, said well we'll haul the chassis up there for 200 dollars, but you don't have to pay the surcharge, that's great, the customer never did have to pay the surcharge according to Interstate Commerce Commission, but the carrier did, and the carrier didn't call us in and ask us hey how about splitting it, we'll make it like uh they'll pay half the surcharge and take-even if they'd have took the 36 dollars off the 200 dollars and still gave us the surcharge it would have looked good, but when they take it away and you know they're doing it illegally, they took the surcharge away from the drivers, they only gave us a flat 250, see, so anyway rather than get involved in that again I said well I let them go 3 trips and then they made a mistake and overpaid me a hundred

dollars, I said well they—I'd—I'd run 3 trips like that, so it was 90—90 dollars plus 18 is 108 dollars, I got a hundred of it back on another mistake that they made, and said rather than go through—like I said I don't want to be a damn uh crusader against every company, and it would be every company because none of them comply. (ABC and XYZ are pseudonyms).

This story, which opens up some other interesting issues that aren't treated here, illustrates that though the regulation has changed, the frame still applies with some changes in low-level detail. As another example, consider this passage from *Overdrive,* a widely-read owner-operator magazine:

Independent truckers will certainly be much better off with the new mileage formula than if the fuel surcharge was dropped with nothing to replace it. But our initial impressions of the mileage-based formula show that many of the same problems, all too prevalent with the fuel surcharge program, will remain (*Overdrive,* 1981, p. 42).

In fairness to the carriers, who are undergoing their own struggle for survival because of regulatory reform and the recession, several stories were told that illustrate implementation of the new mileage compensation program in a straightforward and honest way. But the meeting I attended, the recorded career history interviews, and discussions in owner-operator magazines, all indicate that there is still frequent experiential evidence for the frame's logic. The change in regulations, for all the good intentions to increase support for owner-operators at the ICC, missed some of the core problems revealed by the thematic analysis. I don't know the regulatory field adequately to argue whether the core problems can be handled with federal regulation or not; but the analysis of themes in hearing transcripts at least shows how some of them are viewed by interest groups and what things about the world would have to change so that they no longer apply.

REFERENCES

Agar, M., & J. Hobbs. (1983). Natural plans. *Ethos, 11,* 33–48.
Bilmes, J. (1981). Proposition and confrontation in legal discussion. *Semiotica, 34,* 251–275.
Interstate Commerce Commission. (1978). The independent trucker: Nationwide survey of owner-operators. Washington, DC: Author.
Interstate Commerce Commission. (1979). The independent trucker: Follow-up survey of owner-operators. Washington, DC. Author.
Maister, D.H. (1980). Management of owner-operator fleets. Lexington, MA: Lexington Books.
Messerschmidt, D.A. (1981). On anthropology "at home." In D.A. Messerschmidt (Ed.), *Anthropologists at home in North America.* Cambridge: Cambridge University Press.
Shuy, R.W. (1982). Topic as the unit of analysis in a criminal law case. In D. Tannen (Ed.), *Analyzing discourse: Text and talk.* Washington, DC: Georgetown University Press.

Part IV

LANGUAGE AND POWER
IN EVERYDAY LIFE

Chapter 8

Analytic Ambiguities in the Communication of Familial Power

Hervé Varenne
Teachers College, Columbia University

It is said that the exact recording of a conversation which had seemed brilliant later gives the impression of indigence. The truth lies here. The conversation reproduced exactly is no longer what it was while we were living it...The conversation no longer exists. It does not ramify in all directions—it *is,* flattened out in the single dimension of sound. Instead of summoning our whole being, it does no more than touch us lightly by ear. (Merleau-Ponty, 1973 [1969], p. 65)

POWER, CONFLICT AND COMMUNICATION ANALYSIS

The early work on communicational analysis[1] has left us with much that will remain central to our work for years to come. It has also left us with certain pretheoretical assumptions. For various historical reasons, the first social scientists to become interested in communicational analysis did so from the

This paper is a moment in a long-term project which I am conducting with Clifford Hill. We are jointly exploring a theme which we introduced in an earlier paper (Hill & Varenne, 1981). We are particularly interested in the interplay between the form of language and the possible "meanings" which participants may be trying to express and which may be assigned to them by analysts. The many conversations I have had with Clifford Hill, the many occasions when we have jointly taught this material are an integral part of this paper. Both us want to thank "Connie" wholeheartedly for the help she gave us by opening her family to us. I also want to thank Ray McDermott. A paper about family interaction cannot be independent of the author's personal familial experiences: Susan, David, Michael, and Catherine Varenne (and Jean, Liliane, Patrick) are very much in the background. I will always be grateful to all of them for the altogether optimistic light in which I see "familial conflict."

[1] The work I am reporting on here could also be glossed as work in "conversational" or "discourse" analysis. Each of these labels evoke different schools of research. All have much in common to the extent that they are all interested in language as used in everyday life. I use the term "communicational analysis" here to emphasize my conviction that the work directly influenced by Bateson is the most useful for the understanding of language use.

point of view of emerging problems in various types of psychoanalytic theory and practice. We have three famous bits of therapeutic conversations, the one reported by Pittenger, Hockett, and Danehy (1960), the one reported by Scheflen (1973), and the one reported by Labov and Fanshel (1977). Behind this published work stands the work done by Bateson and the Palo Alto group (McQuown, 1971). What has emerged from it is Birdwhistell's analysis of a male lighting a cigarette for a female (Birdwhistell, 1970). The research itself sprang from an interest in pathological familial environments around Bateson's double-bind theory (1972). The relevance of the famous "cigarette scene" in fact lies in the beginning of the demonstration that the apparently most innocent gestures carry with them the whole structural history of an institutional interactional pattern. It has been difficult for communicational analysis to find application outside of psychoanalysis, though we now have a number of analyses in settings, particularly school or school-like, where psychopathology is not the apparent main concern (Goodwin, 1981; McDermott, 1977; McDermott & Gospodinoff, 1979; Mehan, 1979; Erikson & Shultz, 1982).

It remains that this shift has not been a shift to settings where there are no interactional problems explicitly labeled in the native system. If the first generation of work sprang from a "native" interest in mental health problems, most of the second generation work springs from a political interest in failures to achieve a state of social harmony, consensus, and mutual understanding. The researchers are driven by an interest that is also a mandate from the society at large. As we move to new settings, such as family environments, the same kind of "problem-solving" mandate requires of us that we focus on well-labeled problems. One of them concerns "relative familial power." This concern has appeared in our cultural consciousness with the growth of feminism and we, as researchers, are expected to provide the relevant knowledge. There is much less of a political mandate for the study of the "normal." And yet, how else can we learn about the "problematical" if not by knowing the nonproblematical? Could it also be that our native identification of the problematic is itself a problem of which we are only vaguely aware?

Besides the push of the cultural mandates, there may also be a more fundamental theoretical logic to the traditional interest in conflict. It may be that either (a) social interaction is an inherently violent process or, (b) the method of communicational analysis is so designed as to color any interaction blood red. In the first case, we would have a fact of (social) nature. In the later case, we would have a methodological artifact.

Social interaction may always be a matter of individual egoisms struggling to achieve their goals in ways that are barely "mitigated." It may also be a matter of cooperation (Grice, 1975, 1978) and trust (Garfinkel, 1963) that sometimes gets out of hand. But cooperation is, also, "collusion," the word McDermott and Tylbor prefer (this volume). Though the Latin root of the word would make it mean "to play together," its modern connotations are not so benign. In any event, it is clear that, by emphasizing uncertainty in the progression of the interaction, the very technique of communicational analysis has a built-in tendency to make it look as if interlocutors were struggling. Pittenger et al., in the first published communicational analysis, already warned future practitioners with the graphic sentence: "One must not mistake the five-inch model for the fly itself" (1960, p. 249). When one brings this recognition of what happens in the analytic process together with a fundamental pessimism about human interaction, one can be led, as Labov and Fanshel were, to argue that it is unethical to conduct communicational analyses on certain kinds of situations, particularly familial ones (1977, p. 352–354). They tell us, in effect, "human interaction does look like a fly. Flies are bothersome enough as they are. Let us not scare outselves to death (or divorce...) by making five-inch scale models."

I am concerned in this paper with the analysis of violence and power struggles in a setting where interpersonal tensions do not have—at a common sense level—the implications they have in interactions where we know about the presence of a massive, diagnosed mental health problem. Such a setting is the "family" in routine everyday life. It is not so much that, in "normal" family life, people do not struggle, suffer and, particularly in the middle-class American world, end up in various types of therapy and divorce. It is rather that such difficulties, including divorce, are incommensurable to other types. To equate routine family difficulties with the type of mental illness that require medication and institutionalization is to trivialize the latter. There is much, however, that can be learned about violence and power by looking at conflicts that are not radically destructive. In particular, we can learn about the analytic processes that allow us to conduct analyses of activities like the exercise of power which must always involve some conflict.

Since power is a social event, it is also a communicational one. It is patterned, structured. As G.H. Mead taught us, a conflict is conflict only to the extent that all protagonists participate actively in it (1934, p. 63). We could even reverse Mauss's analysis of gift giving as a coercive social fact ([1923–4] 1967) and see in conflict a moment of social cooperation when two apparently distinct protagonists get together to do something that is well organized by some "shared" pattern. There is a ritual frame to conflict that will also have to be understood.

Power, however, can be exercised at times when it is not the main "topic" of the interaction. Indeed, the peculiar exercise of power through discourse interests us all the more that the conflict has not been brought to the explicit awareness of the participants in the specific discourse which we are analyzing. Most participants can make various kinds of what Silverstein calls "metapragmatic" statements about interaction (1981). They can negotiate the actual pragmatics of their interaction in metapragmatic conversations.

The kind of Americans that this paper is about are in fact extremely expert at such conversations. The goal of our research in the exercise of power in everyday life is not, however, to rely on such moments, or even to make much of them.[2] It is rather to focus on moments when the metapragmatics of the interaction are not on the floor explicitly even though what is being performed would appear as exemplary tokens in metapragmatic statements of power—as they indeed are in this paper. Power is exercised when a mugger points a gun at a jogger and asks for his wallet. Power is exercised when a woman asks her husband for three dollars to buy milk. Power is also exercised when this woman complains *about* her husband making her ask for grocery money. "Power," however, is not "on the floor" in the same manner in each instance. We must be able to handle the difference. I will talk of the behavioral manifestations that allow us to talk of "power" even when it is not explicitly on the floor as "markers" that can be qualified as "diacritical" markers in that they are performed "on top of," or "around" the main surface markers that define the event as what it is within the overall frame of everyday life.

That conflict should be marked behaviorally must mean that there must be times when the markers are absent. To see conflict, we must also see nonconflict in the behavioral stream. Historically, the analysis of nonconflict has been the hardest to conduct. The interest of the analysts has been most typically with the demonstration that large interactional problems are mirrored, if not caused, in the detail of apparently nonconflictual moments. This argument was based on the structuralist principle that any moment in the operation of a system necessarily summarizes the operating mechanisms of the whole. Inappropriately handled, this argument can also dissolve internal differentiation into entropic sameness. It must be clearly realized that, in structuralist theory, systemic organization is based upon differentiation at the next lower level. To look at the organization of conflict in an interaction, it is necessary to search for the alternation between conflictual and nonconflictual moments as these are marked by the presence or absence of the appropriate markers.[3]

We must in fact go further if we want to look at any specific interaction *in the context* of other interactions (rather than only "as" a context for bits

---

[2] It is also a serious error not to delve into the metapragmatic awareness of the participants. It is also a very difficult task that is becoming urgent if we are to understand the pragmatic structures themselves. Above all, we must accept that the making of a metapragmatic statement "about" a pragmatic usage does not terminate the research. It confronts us with a new problem to investigate since the tie between a statement and its metapragmatic twin is always semiotic, never referential.

[3] Bateson himself understood these structuralist principles well. His analysis of the alcoholic is exemplary: Alcoholism is *one* pattern ("once an alcoholic, always an alcoholic—even when apparently sober") that consists of the *alteration* between two states, sobriety and drunkenness, both of which are clearly marked.

of behavior within the scene). In order to be recognizable as a specific kind of scene, rather than another, any interaction must be marked. In other words, "putting-the-children-to-bed-while-cooking-dinner" is a different kind of moment in a family's life from "doing-homework," or from "talking-about-marriage." While we do not yet have many analyses of family life that even begin to catalogue the set of differentiated moments that the family and the culture hold the members accountable for performing, there is little doubt that such analyses are possible and needed.[4] The markers of "kind of setting" must thus be performed concurrently with the markers of "conflict." In fact, the people must *concurrently* perform many kinds of markers relevant to *different* systems of signification or accountability. The analytic question which we are left with now concerns the grounds on which we could decide that any one of these structures of markers is "the" structure of the interaction. I want to suggest that we cannot settle such an investigation. It is more promising, and corresponds more closely to the activity we wish to understand, to see any diacritic marker as justification for the *possibility* of an analysis given a setting marked for the relevance of the markers.

Concretely, it is possible that the markers of conflict are only relevant *as such* in settings where something can be made of them, for example, perhaps those moments in family life when two protagonists hold each other accountable to "fighting" (a pragmatic setting), and those moments when we, sometimes as natives, and sometimes as scholarly analysts, tell each other about conflict (metapragmatic settings). Theoretically, this position is a development on something that was very well put by Pittenger and his colleagues. "In theory," they wrote, "the relative importance of a single event can be assayed by observing how far its effects 'reverberate' up through more and more inclusive larger events of which it is a constituent" (1960, p. 250). What is interesting about conflict markers is that they may have radically different effects on larger events depending on the overall definition of that larger event. I show in this paper how markers of conflict can be performed that have no immediate impact upon an interaction while they can also be seen as symptomatic of serious problems *but only in another setting*.

ONE FAMILY IN CONVERSATION

In this paper, I look contrastively at the few moments when it can be said plausibly that tension emerges in a half-hour recording of familial conversa-

---

[4] For the beginning of such analyses see Varenne, Hamid-Buglione, McDermott, & Morison (1982) and Varenne and McDermott (1986) in which are explored the structural markers of "doing-homework." While the language adopted there and in this paper is most directly related to the ethnomethodological phrasings of Garfinkel (1967) as these can be understood in the context of Bateson's earlier work, it should be noted that these phrasings are not epistemologically different from those that are favored in the European linguistic structuralism of Jakobson and Levi-Strauss.

tion.[5] The recording was made by a woman, Connie Harvey, in her home. It was early evening on a school night. Around her were her two young children, Mike and Kate. Her husband, Ray (Mike and Kate's father), and her son by a first marriage, Jack, also actively participated in the activities. During the half hour quite a lot of ground was covered: Ray, Connie, and Jack talked about incidents in their respective day, Mike finished his homework, Connie sewed, Ray and she talked about a piece of furniture they might buy; they began cooking the dinner and organizing the children for a prebedtime reading session. Connie's initial interpretation[6] of the evening, when she gave us the tape and began helping us transcribe, was that "nothing happened." Much later, when we talked to her about our preliminary analyses which showed that, on the contrary, much had been going on, she remained doubtful. Even though she had labored hard to help us transcribe, she had forgotten much of what had happened. This was a very unmemorable evening.

This interpretation by a participant is central and it must remain with us as we start blowing up portions of the recording and "make a five-inch model of the fly." As we see presently, it is easiest *for us* to write a statement that looks like an "interpretation" of any sequence within the conversation in a mode that emphasizes the negative, the tense, the aggressive. It is much harder to write in a mode that emphasizes the positive, the cooperative, the sharing. These initial, gut reactions to the transcripts were strong enough to make me wonder whether, after all, Labov and Fanshel were not right in saying that one should not study family conversations for ethical reasons. What I saw was symptomatic of the kinds of interactional patterns which, after interpretation, and in the cultural context of upper-middle-class-professional Manhattan, can be used as justification for divorce. When we found out that, two years later, Ray and Connie had gotten a divorce, it was hard not to claim a kind of foreknowledge. All this makes it even more imperative that we do not easily dismiss the statements that Connie made both before and after the divorce that, at the time when the

---

[5] The corpus on which Clifford Hill and I are working consists of:
1. one hour of pre-bedtime talk recorded by Connie Harvey. A detailed, timed, transcript of the verbalization has been established. The first half-hour has also been analyzed for the explicit emergence of "activities" (≠ topics);
2. one hour of "historical" interview, done two months after the original tape, to establish the referents of elliptical statements;
3. two hours of "psychodynamic" interviews, done two years later. Rough transcripts of these tapes have been established.

[6] In fact, this "interpretation" should be introduced as what Burke called a (rhetorical) "identification" (1969: 20): it is a gloss on something that happened some time in the past, made in a different setting, to a different audience, with a vocabulary that is not the one that could have been used in the original setting.

recording was made, divorce was not at all in the cards. Connie, at that time, could not make the type of statements which I could make. Two years later, she still felt that these statements were forced. For her, I was then, and am still, making much too much out of what she heard herself say. If there was a tempest that night, it was in a teapot. We may not agree with her but we must also recognize that her denial is an analytic problem which cannot be resolved by reference to "repression." Even if Connie was repressing reality, we must ask ourselves what it was, in the interaction and its context, which allowed her to repress.

It is necessary first, briefly, to outline the incident around which this analysis centers. The recording happened to start just before Ray came into the room on his return from work and shopping. His first words concern his finding that day an object which remains unspecified ("a proper china thing"—see Text 1, below). Connie answers "I don't believe it" and moves on into along explanation of what she had done about the kitchen sink, into which, the day before, Ray's wedding ring had fallen. Ray participates in this conversation. At the end, after a brief silence, Connie says "Tell me about the china closet," thereby demonstrating that she had picked up on Ray's initial statement. She is immediately interrupted by her son Jack with whom she starts a conversation expanding on something that was implied in the discussion of the sink repair. This is followed by an indirect reinstatement of the cabinet topic by Ray. Connie picks up on it but she and Ray soon (after one minute) drop it as the children call to them. It is only eight minutes later that the parents can have a sustained (four minutes) exchange about the cabinet. They also have another brief exchange about it twenty minutes later. This extremely interrupted process has in fact accomplished much. By the end of the half-hour we know what Ray found, Connie's opinion of this finding, and what she would like to have happen:

1. Ray found a china cabinet to display a nice Tiffany china bought at the time of the wedding, ten years earlier, and ever since stored in boxes; this cabinet is fifteen inches deep and eighty-one inches high; it has glass shelves and an oriental top; it's lit from inside; its color is light; it is one thousand dollars and it could not be delivered for two months;
2. Connie is not enthusiastic; she is particularly skeptical about the color; she wants to see it before it is bought.

There is a disagreement here that gets negotiated. This disagreement, however, is not directly brought to the floor (Connie is never explicitly negative about the cabinet). To understand the depth of this disagreement other matters must be mentioned. Connie told us soon after the recording was made that this was about the first time in their married life that Ray had gone shopping for household furniture. Until then the household had been Connie's sole responsibility. She had come to resent this. They had talked about it and had expliticly decided that Ray should take more responsibility. This was the first time he exercised this responsibility. Much more than a cabinet was thus at stake.

What is at stake seems to get rather sharply drawn when one looks at the exact pattern of the interactions around the cabinet discussion. Many of the interruptions mentioned earlier are the products of the fact that the other persons in the situation were entitled to the floor, were not interested in the cabinet discussion, and imposed their own interests. In general, no topic ever held the stage for longer than a few minutes—even though most topics were repeatedly recycled. It would thus have been difficult, if not impossible, for Ray and Connie to have a sustained conversation about the cabinet the first time Ray introduced the topic. To do so would have violated the conversational rules that typified this family. The shift in topic, however, must itself get accomplished. It is the manner of this accomplishment that is revealing.

Let us look, for example, at two of the junctions when Ray and Connie drop the cabinet:

TEXT 1[7]

	Ray	Mike	Connie	Kate	Jack
15—	.well				
16—	Connie I think I		. [+ + + + + + + + + +		
17—	found us our thing		h + + + + + + + + + +/]		
18—	today/		. you did		
19—			what? .		
20—	. found us				
21—	uuh				
22—	. a proper				
23—	china thing/				
24—			I don't believe		
25—			it/.		
26—			. I told Mary		
27—			to look for your ring/		

---

[7] The following transcription conventions are relevant here: (a) Each person' speech is transcribed in a vertical column; (b) each line of the transcript represents a second (numbered on the left); (c) one dot within a line (e.g., second 15, 16, 18, 19., etc., indicates a pause of half a second); (d) normal orthography is used throughout (no attempt is made to display accents or intonational patterns); (e) an "/" indicates the end of an utterance (falling intonation) except if the utterance ends as a question or an exclamation; (f) an "-" indicates a stutter; (g) underlining indicates a strong emphasis.

TEXT 2

	Ray	Mike	Connie	Kate	Jack
231—	. he				
232—	probably could get				
233—	this thing				
234—	for zilch money/				
235—					
236—			Mommy/		
237—					
238—	. + −		. I could		
239—	. it's a		build it/.		
240—	thousand dollars/		. Jack		
241—			honey,		
242—			. Mike		
243—			has-got a-large		
244—			load of crayons,		
245—			in the cement		
246—			mixer/		
247—					
248—					
249—					
250—	. Mike/		. Jack/		
251—	I brought you				
252—	a present/				
253—		. what .			

Text 1 is particularly interesting for the fact that the shift in topic (from cabinet to sink) may in fact not be a shift at all: Both topics have to do with the performance of household chores. Furthermore, what emerges most clearly in the sink exchanges is Ray's incompetence: he suggested that the janitor get the gold ring with a magnet. It is altogether not very "nice" of Connie to remind him of this statement (though he picks it up as a good joke). It is even less nice if we see in this story an implicit commentary on his statement that he found the proper cabinet: *"I don't believe you are competent to find such a cabinet."[8]

The movement out of the cabinet in Text 2 is more complex. A minute earlier, Ray had asked Connie for the address of a couple they had once met. Thirty seconds later, we can begin to suspect what is the relevance of this search. Ray says "[Jim] is in the furniture business." Thirty more seconds pass during which Ray and Connie continue to discuss where they might

---

[8] An asterisk in front of a statement in quote marks (*"...") indicates that the statements has not in fact been produced by the participants. It is our version of what might also have been said.

find the address until Ray restates "anyhow he's in the furniture business"
and adds "he probably could get this thing for zilch money" (sec. 231).
Notice that the "thing" is not specified. In fact, Ray never refers to the
cabinet by name. Only Connie does. But she is never confused by his mode
of reference. Then, in less than ten seconds, two important statements are
made which begin to specify what is going on. Connie appears to grab onto
Ray's "zilch money" to state something to the effect that, after all, she—an
amateur—could "build it." Given the earlier emphasis on the fact that the
cabinet found is a "proper" one (sec. 22), it is easy to see a challenge here.
It is easy also to see in Ray's "it's a thousand dollars" a denial of Connie's
suggestion (a) that she could build it and (b) that Ray cannot find a "proper"
cabinet. It is tempting to see a pattern here. It would be made up of:

1.   Ray's assertions;

followed by:

2.   Connie's challenges of the grounds for Ray's assertions;

sometimes followed by:

3.   Ray's defenses.

As we see presently, this progression is repeated several times that evening.
    In any event, and even before Ray has finished making his statement
about the worth of the cabinet, Connie turns towards the children and one
of their immediate concerns. For at least three minutes, the younger children have tried to get one of the parents' attention, though without explicit
insistence. Mike's "mommy" (Text 2, sec. 236) was but the latest in a series.
The issue, which the parents asserted visually, was Mike's inability to get
crayons out of a toy cement-mixer truck. Connie turns to Jack. In view of
the preceding exchanges about fixing the sink, it may not be irrelevant that
Connie calls for Jack rather than her husband to make a little bit of household repair. In any event, Ray does not pick up on the "interruption" as an
interruption (in other words he does not say anything like: *"Connie, I am
talking to you. Can't the children wait?") He joins Connie. At this point
(sec. 250), they are in a perfect, multi-level synchrony. They start together,
each address a child in a complementary manner: Connie asks for the repair;
Ray seeks to distract Mike while the repair is being made. But is it enough to
say that the cabinet topic is dropped? Isn't it possible that the shift from
cabinet to helping the children is itself significant as a statement about the
cabinet and the interaction?

I will not attempt this analysis here. I just want to suggest the complexity of the interaction and the difficulty we would encounter if we tried to analyze fully these exchanges. Undoubtedly, there is tension. There is also a high level of cooperation in the Gricean sense. It seems easy for Ray and Connie to enter into temporal synchrony. Again and again we see them starting to speak together thereby revealing that they are rhythmically together.[9] It happens twice in Text 2 (sec. 238 and 250). This is all the more surprising given the radical differences in the tempo of their speech and the time interval which each needs between utterances: her speech has a rapid halting tempo and she finds it easy to start either slightly before the end of another's speech or with it. Ray, on the contrary, is quite slow. He has a strong tendency to overarticulate and needs at least a second, if not more, after the end of one of his, or somebody else's utterances, before he can start to speak. Altogether, he speaks much less than Connie. She repeatedly rides over him (e.g. Text 2, sec. 238). At such times there never seems to be explicit struggles for the floor. These, at least, do not surface. At other times the whole family seems to organize itself to give Ray all the time he needs.

The harmony that all this suggests may even be more encompassing. An analysis of the whole half hour shows that every member of the household is given the chance of completing one or more sequences centering on a personal interest. Besides the china cabinet discussion, we have extended consideration of:

- a gift for Mike
- a birthday party for Kate
- a band rehearsal for Jack
- Mike's homework which gets done
- Connie sewing
- the cooking of the dinner meal in which Ray is directly involved
- two other incidents in Connie's day

All these activities are accomplished in the same interrupted pattern which we mentioned when talking about the way the cabinet was discussed, but, in each case, we could see that the conversations were progressing. This is anything but a broken or dysfunctional family.

We mentioned earlier that few interactional analyses emphasize harmony. An interesting exception is Erickson's work (1982) on a dinner conversation which he ends on a display of the music-like pattern of the people's interactions. They may have been disputing, but they were also doing it in a

---

[9] The importance of this observation cannot be overemphasized if we are looking for physical evidence of their communicational togetherness (Byers, 1976).

graceful dance. At least as much could be said about the family under consideration here. As we move on to look at the two instances of explicit para-
verbal aggravation to be found in the half hour, we must keep this in mind.

MULTIPLE PERFORMANCES OF AGGRAVATION

The first instance of aggravation occurs during the main cabinet discussion.
At minute 10, Connie said "Could you- let us hear more about the china
cabinet." This followed a request from Ray for a "tape measure" while he
moved furniture about. At the same time however, Jack had asked for the
newspaper. During the first minute there is thus a movement back and forth
between the cabinet and the newspaper made even more complex by a co-
occurent search conducted by Kate for dress snaps in Connie's sewing box.
Connie is at the center of these three activities and is, at least implicitly, held
accountable by the other three for paying attention to their interests. Earlier
on, it seemed that Ray and Connie, in such a situation, would retreat and
deal with the children's interest leaving behind their own. Indeed they have
been with the children for the preceding six minutes, dealing with crayons,
gifts, a pouting child, a birthday party, homework, preparation for bed,
and reading.

This time, however, Ray does not yield the floor. We suspect that some
visual clues may have served to signal this refusal. In any event, after Connie's
instructions to Jack regarding the location of the paper, she, and all the
other participants, give Ray the second-and-a-half silence that he needs to
start an utterance. As usual, he is totally elliptical:

TEXT 3

Ray	Mike	Connie	Kate	Jack
619— that's thiirty				
620— six and a half/				
621— and that's				
622— thirty six				
623— o K?				
624—				
625—		yeeah/		
626—		. and how		
627—		*deep* is it?		
628—		. is it		
629—		deep enough to hold		
630—		the-the large		
631— *Welll/*		dish? .		
632— . the thing				
633— is we may				
634— have to do				

TEXT 3 (Continued)

Ray	Mike	Connie	Kate	Jack
635— some *slan*ting				
636— and stuff				
637— like that/				
638— uhm-				
639—				
640—		. find it?		
641—		he found the		
642—		paper/		
643—				
644— . fif				
645— teen deep/				
646—				
647—				
648—				
649— which means it				
650— would come ouut				
651— toooo				
652— . here/				
653—				
654—				
655— Connie		maybe maybe		
656—		maybe down in		
657—		the end of this		
658—		drawer		
659— . Connie!		even .	.+ + + + +	
660— it's three			+ + + + + + + +	
661— inches				
662— deeep				
663—			+ + + + + + + +	

As far as we could figure it out, the first "that" refers to a space in the living room and the other to the size of the cabinet. Certainly, Connie understands the reference to her satisfaction. She immediately questions Ray about another descriptive characteristic of the cabinet: its depth. He answers. She shifts to still another characteristic: the height, then the style of the top, then the color. However, she is still monitoring Jack's search for the paper and Kate's search for the snaps. This does not deter Ray. Rather, he starts to perform things which he has not yet done that half hour: he begins to bracket his utterances about the cabinet with words like "o K" (rising inflection on the K) "welll," "uhm-." Something different is happening which Connie seems to understand as a sign that he is not ready to relinquish the floor. She continually returns to the cabinet, though apparently in such an ambiguous fashion that Ray calls out to her twice "Connie," "Connie!" (at sec. 655 and 659). The second call has the clear intonational contour of mild aggravation.

What is interesting here is that this aggravation is not solely suggested by the way certain statements are arranged. It is explicitly performed. It is very much there. And for the following two minutes, all of Connie's utterances directly concern the cabinet. In fact, at sec. 674, soon after Ray's outburst, she states "I'm interested." This seems redundant given that she is now in her questioning mode which could be considered enough to demonstrate this interest. Her statement is an expansion of the obvious. It is appealing to see in this response a reaction to the aggravation.

As mentioned earlier, this part of the cabinet discussion ends with a discussion of delivery dates and is punctuated by Connie's final "I'm not in a hurry. What's the hurry?" It is quite clear by then that Connie is not enthusiastic if not outright negative about the cabinet described. She has stopped questioning Ray. Four times, consecutively, she only responds to a descriptive statement with a low "oooh" (with a downward intonation). In apparent response, Ray's descriptions become less and less fluent, more elliptical and halting. Connie's disapproval is not, however, explicitly marked as such. It is not picked up by Ray as a refusal. What is picked up is the end-of-discussion marker performed by Connie. Ray and Connie both now turn towards Kate and resolve her search for the snaps.

This is soon followed by Ray's introduction of a new topic: He takes out of a paper bag some Indian foods which he bought on his way home. In a singsong voice he says "I went to India today! got mom's favorite goodies." Connie reacts to this with laughter and exited intonations: "Good! Oh, I'm happy. It's time we had curry." In less than thirty seconds, the mood has completely changed, apparently. As usual, the focus on the food is interrupted by the children. Connie begins to talk to Jack about a band rehearsal. Then, in the middle of a sentence addressed to Jack (sec. 1023), "out of the blue," she interrupts herself and admonishes her husband in a way redundantly marked for disapproval (sec. 1025 to 1029):

TEXT 4

Ray	Mike	Connie	Kate	Jack
1015—		Andrew		
1016—		knew what		
1017—		hours		
1018—		the practice		
1019—		would be?		
1020—				
1021—				
1022—		because he's		
1023—		one of the- .		
1024—				
1025—		Ray I think		
1026—		you got		
1027—		too hot!		

TEXT 4 (Continued)

Ray	Mike	Connie	Kate	Jack
1028—		it's		
1029—		too hot/		
1030— honey!				
1031—				
1032— we said				
1033— we'd get				
1034— *hot*!				

Connie does not continue and this is the end (?) of it. The few further passing references to the Indian foods occur in a neutral mode.

PERFORMANCE AND CONVERSATIONAL PREMISES ("PROPOSITIONS")

The above analyses are mainly intended to be suggestive of the analytic difficulties that confront us. What is certain is that, within the same family, within the same scene, the expression of conflict can be systematically varied by manipulating the various expressive mechanisms available to the participants. Ray and Connie can express disapproval either by dropping a topic, denying the relevance of an apparently secondary element of the topic (e.g., can Connie "build" the cabinet?), calling for focused attention, all the way to explicitly expanding on the mistake ("You got it too hot!"). As we presently see, this variation in the expression may be but a surface manifestation of an overarching conflict over household management. However, this overarching conflict is not explicitly referred to. In another setting, this conflict could be expanded much further. There is thus still further possible alternations which contrastively mark the setting we are looking at as a particular kind of setting.[10]

What I want to do here is focus upon the analytic process that would allow us to go further than the sketch of a description which I just presented. It would seem an easy task to relate the minor clashes I have depicted to an ongoing power struggle between Ray and Connie around the conduct of the household and, through it, around their respective "roles." It would seem even easier then to relate this personal struggle between the two of them to the larger struggle which, supposedly, the sexes have been fighting for a

---

[10] Clifford Hill and I are preparing a paper that will focus explicitly upon the marking qualities of the fact that the "same" event can be expanded in radically "different" manners. It seems as if the ability to expand something in a particular direction is one of the symbolic behaviors that can mark a scene as what it is ("putting-the-children-to-bed" vs. "talking-about-the-marriage," for example).

very long time. Such arguments have been made many times and I would not contribute much by restating them. What I will do now first is to retrace the grounds on which such an argument could be made in order to show the type of transformations which would have to be done on the text as performed before it could be made to fit within a "power struggles within the family" discourse.

The first step in an analysis of the overall interactional structure that may underlie what we have just described would probably start with a stress on the extent to which the pattern of the "Indian food" exchange duplicates the pattern of the cabinet discussion: Ray states that he did something competently, Connie points out that he did not. In the last case, Ray explicitly rebels. The rebellion was less clearly marked in the cabinet discussion—though his calls to order may be an aspect of this rebellion. We would also mention as relevant that, later, Ray did buy an expensive ("proper"?) china cabinet (though not the one discussed the night we taped), that he did so without consulting Connie (and gave it to her on her birthday), and that she told us that she did like that one.

Earlier, we summarized the analysis of the initial "cabinet" sequence with a statement that seemed to capture the implicit "message" that Connie might be sending. All her responses to Ray around the cabinet seem to say: *"I don't believe you are competent to find a proper cabinet." It would be easy to elevate this statement to the level of what Labov and Fanshel call a "proposition." The statement appears to refer to "the cognitive component of conversational transactions...what may be defined as...what is 'really being talked about'" (1977, p. 52). My instinct here is to be much more conservative about the referential value of the proposition. Nobody could be certain that "competence" is what is really being talked about—not even the participants who could not possibly be truthful about it. On the other hand "propositions" have an evocative value which make them useful in analytic discussion. I construct the rest of this discussion around such propositional statements.

We start with the following "local" proposition:

- *Local Proposition 1:* I DO NOT BELIEVE YOU ARE COMPETENT
  TO FIND A PROPER CABINET

On the same grounds we may add another local one:

- *Local Proposition 2:* I DO NOT BELIEVE YOU ARE COMPETENT
  TO SHOP FOR INDIAN FOODS

Using a familiar process of abstraction in which one changes content words by words that refer to the general category to which these words belong, we may write the following more "general" proposition:

• *General Proposition 1:* YOU ARE NOT COMPETENT TO HANDLE HOUSEHOLD AFFAIRS

To this proposition would correspond Ray's complementary one:

• *General Proposition 2:* I AM COMPETENT IN HOUSEHOLD AFFAIRS

The existence of such a disagreement around competence in handling household affairs could be validated by something Connie told us later in an interview: after several years of housewifery, she protested to Ray that she wanted to get out of the household to complete her education and practice the profession she had been trained for. She wanted him to participate more actively in internal household management. Ray agreed to this, though not without hesitation. In other words, the competence issue is also a participation issue that could be summarized as another general proposition:

• *General Proposition 3:* HUSBAND (DOES NOT) PARTICIPATES IN HOUSEHOLD AFFAIRS

This is a joint general proposition.[11] But it was more in the way of a difficult question than of an easy resolution. Ray's participation was difficult for both of them. Depending on one's point of view, one could see in his relative incompetence (?) a deliberate strategy on his part to be relieved of the responsibility (*"Perhaps you better take care of it since you think I can't handle it"). One could also see it as Connie placing him in a Catch-22: *"You must participate, you can't participate."

It is an easy step from the observation of "disagreements" about a state of affairs to a blank statement to the effect that this disagreement is symptomatic of an "underlying conflict." Furthermore, these difficulties have a familiar ring to us all in this day and age. Ray and Connie's problem is one that faces most of us in the upper middle classes. And many of us have dealt with it in ways that have led to conflict and, indeed, divorce. Even if we knew nothing about Ray and Connie, we would still be able, by simple virtue of being actors in recent American culture, to participate in a conversation based on the premise that PARTICIPATION IN HOUSEHOLD AFFAIRS is something that is "a source of conflict" that can escalate to divorce, the ultimate in familial discord. I want to stress here that this ability to participate in such a conversation is not something which we gained from the analysis of the case under study here. It is extraneous to it, and yet so broadly relevant to it that even Connie, in later interviews, could actually make the

---

[11] There is much evidence that this is also a "cultural" proposition, a model "of" and 'for" behavior, as Geertz put it (1973, p. 93–94).

same point. This suggests that a full analysis of the interactions we looked at should include a statement of the cultural logic which makes such disputes, when generalized, relevant to divorce. This could be stated as a kind of "cultural proposition":

- *Cultural Proposition 1:* THE RELATIVE PARTICIPATION OF SPOUSES IN HOUSEHOLD AFFAIRS IS A CENTRAL ELEMENT IN THE DECISION TO REMAIN MARRIED

This is the proposition which allows people in the United States to have conversations about cases such as the one we are looking at. It makes sense of such cases in settings such as this paper (and many others, of course).

On the same grounds that allowed us to draw the cultural proposition, a discussion of "power" could be made relevant to our case. Power is not immediately at issue at the surface of the text as performed. To bring it in we must rely on another kind of extraneous knowledge, a kind to which I will refer as "theoretical." Many of us can easily participate in conversations based on the premise that disagreements about participation and competence in household affairs is a matter of "power struggles." We easily operate on the principle that persons inevitably have different interests, that certain events favor one type of interest more than another type, that interacting persons will struggle to see their self-interests win, and "might makes right," in a Hobbesian war of "all against all." Such principles make it plausible to say that Ray and Connie are locked in a fight over dominance in household affairs. In this fight, they seem to be using any available resource to win. It would be easy to look again at all the statements we examined to evaluate what kind of weapon they constitute. We would see Ray and Connie use, besides the aggravated attack, the strategic retreat, the indirect challenge, the loving concession to be used as a lever to obtain another concession later, and so on. The "underlying theoretical proposition" could be phrased as follows:

- *Theoretical Proposition 1:* ISSUES OF RELEVANCE TO THE STABILITY OF INSTITUTIONALIZED INTERACTION MAY BE LOOKED AT IN TERMS OF RELATIVE POWER OF THE PARTICIPANTS

To do the above would be consistent both with what the participants can themselves perform (though in other settings) and with what the sociological tradition has taught us. In the subsequent interviews which I had with Connie, she found it easy to talk about power struggles, the means used, and the possible "winner" of these strategies. The sociological tradition would similarly suggest that, to get into the realms of "Power" or "Interactional Patterns" (as theoretical terms), is to reach the end point of one's analysis. We could argue that we have now described "what was really going on" and that we have reached a "deep structure" of the family's interaction. These statements would then be the referent of any future analysis. We would stop being interested in "china closets" and would only talk about "difficult conflicts around the issue of dealing with household affairs."

- Is this a valid end point?
- Do interactions HAVE structures?
- What did happen that evening?

THE CULTURAL STRUCTURING OF ANALYTIC CONVERSATIONS

These are classical problems in anthropology. Replace the word "interaction" with the word "society" and we find ourselves in the midst of the old debate between Radcliffe-Brown ([1940] (1965) and Lévi-Strauss ([1952] 1962, 1953) about the best way of stating how the words "society" and the word "structure" belong together. With Lévi-Strauss, I would prefer to think that societies (and interactions, frames, etc.) are structur*ed* but do not "have" structures. The search must be for structur*ing* principles. In that search it is necessary to deal with all the elements of the event. Nothing that happens is structurally irrelevant and one only abstracts at the risk of losing one's bearing. In our case, the act of digging for the deep structure clearly had the tendency of making us lose sight of the fact that *no fundamental challenge of the marriage occurred that evening*. The challenge may have been close to the co-occurrent mental speech of the participants. It may have been "unconscious" (as we would have to say if we took seriously Connie's statement to the effect that "nothing" had happened that night). But it did not explicitly surface. Even aggravation did not surface often and it was soon buried. To argue that such a muted sound is equivalent to the thunder of a full blown fight is to make one unable to deal with the principles of alternation and contrast which make it possible to distinguish a fight from its nonfight environment. For "nothing to happen" something has to happen: certain kinds of symbolic acts must be performed that signal that, in fact, "nothing is happening." "Nothingness" is a cultural category and its signalling will vary enormously cross-culturally. The quiet, slow, deliberate pace of the Harvey's talk, such facts as the almost complete absence of overlaps, the respect of turn-taking rules, everything that happened that night is functionally arbitrary to "nothing is happening." For nothing to happen, in other cultures, radically different kinds of things would have to have been performed. Conversely, everything that marks the particular evening which we recorded as "uninteresting" must be specified by the analysis rather than abstracted out as a contingent realization of the deep structure.

We cannot, at this stage of the analysis, specify what makes this evening uninteresting. We suspect that, for this family, the absence of aggravation, the avoidance of certain topics or ways of talking about co-occurent events, and so on, had a role to play in the performance of "nothing." But this analysis could not be done in the absence of comparative data: what happens when something happens?

This analysis remains to be done. We can however already suggest some of the things that are implied by the stance which we are taking here. It is not trivial that we could produce general propositions like HUSBAND (DOES NOT) PARTICIPATE IN HOUSEHOLD AFFAIRS. Once we realize that this "is" not the structure *of* the recorded interaction, we must still deal with the fact that this proposition is plausible. It makes sense. In certain settings, Ray and Connie could easily produce a conversation in which the proposition could explicitly be brought up as an issue. The process of such a "meta"- conversation is as concrete as the process of the conversation we glanced at: it happens and can be documented. It will have to be analyzed and this will have to be done *contrastively* to the analysis of the other interactions to which we have the (cultural) feeling that it is referentially "about." What is important here is that the relationship between any interaction (e.g., whether Indian foods are too hot) and any other interaction (e.g., a conversation about who is to buy groceries) is never the simple one that seems to tie a statement to "what it is all about." Potentially at least, anything can be said about something else when that other thing has moved off the floor. However, we can still ask: is the process that gives any proposition its plausibility "free"? In the absolute? In the particular culture of the participants or of the analyst? Can "anything" actually be said?

In fact, I suspect that a lot could be said which could be shown to make some sense in some system. Certainly, the participants would say different things about it than we, as analysts, would. Each of them would vary their statements depending on the situation in which they would have to make them, the relationship they assumed they had with their audience, and so on. Giving the same text to people from other cultures would produce still more surprising statements. The set of all these statements would be miscellaneous indeed! But I suspect also that this set would not be completely miscellaneous. Each text would have to begin with something that was actually performed in the original—whether it was "significant" or not, whether it made a big difference that evening or not. The challenges, the defenses, the exercises in power which we could see in the recording were performed but not "as" challenges, defenses, or power plays. These terms belong to another frame than the one the participants were using that evening. Only cabinets, sinks, crayons, and newspapers could appear in the frame they were using. We must respect this fact. We must also respect the fact that challenges, defenses, and power plays could be made relevant to the setting.

To get out of what seems like an analytic dead end, we need to extend the traditional statements about structural significance. From the beginning, phonology has been based on the analytic principle that not everything that is performed phonetically by a speaker at a particular time is equally significant in any particular reference frame. While linguists have only dealt with sounds in the narrowest sense, the same analytic principles can be seen at play in the work of Labov on the identificatioan of what used to be called "accents" (1972, 1982). If one brings together this work with traditional phonology when analyzing a particular utterance, it can then be seen that, here too, we are in a situation where the same event can be seen to have different properties depending on the analytic point of view chosen. It would be seen clearly that it is not a case of competing interpretations (one right, the other wrong) but rather of the complexity of actual performance.

Complexity itself must be analysed. "Accents" are continually performed, but they are not continually significant. They are only significant at certain times, particularly, perhaps, in interethnic interaction. Isolated communities may not even be aware that "accents" can be relevant. Even in our modern multi-ethnic societies, accents have a very specific kind of relevance. They mark us in certain kinds of interaction. It only takes a very few utterances to identify an accent. About any utterance will do for this identification. Then, no new information can be carried by the presence of the accent except confirmation of the initial identification. In a practical interaction, when more is to be accomplished than ethnic identification, the accent must, and will, cease to be a significant piece of information. It continues to be performed but only as a kind of diacritic marker which can be referred to if need be.

I am attracted by an understanding of the kind of structural interactional redundancy that has fascinated analysts ever since the Palo Alto group started looking at recorded behavior intensively that would follow the same kind of track. The general propositions I abstracted for the Harveys earlier could be seen as a kind of redundancy in the performance of something that is present, but only as a diacritical marker of the same sort as the other markers they also perform which show them to be, for example, New York White Anglo-Saxon Protestants. As diacritical markers, the signs of their way of fighting with each other are definitively there. Any analyst is entitled to look at them as revealing of something that, perhaps, could not be observed any other way (either because it is "unconscious" or because the explicit expansion of the pattern could only occur in the absence of observers

—as marital fights generally are in our society). But they should not be taken as more than diacritical markers in the actual situation in which they were performed.[12]

In conclusion, it seems to me that a power analysis of an interaction is not, strictly speaking, an analysis "of" the interaction. It is, rather, an analysis made *permissible* by the interplay of:

1. an actual performance;

and:

2. a plausibility or coherence system (a "theory," an "ideology" or "culture") which justifies the making of certain statements about certain things.

The coherence system itself is not a product of the instances of the world about which it can be used. It is rather the product of social interaction among a certain group of persons and for some of their purposes—persons and purposes being probably very different from the persons that participated in the original utterance and their purposes. Such a stance may seem to cloud issues of textual interpretations that are already too complex. And yet, there are few among us that do not think that, in a few years, the analyses which have been produced until now will appear massively simplistic, naive, and overly unsystematic. For progress to occur, we must not look ourselves into unwarranted assumptions about relevance or signification. Our only possible route is the one that takes us back to the text as performed in all its wealth of potentialities.

REFERENCES

Bateson, G. (1972). *Steps to an ecology of the mind.* New York: Ballantine Books.
Birdwhistell, R. (1970). *Kinesics and context: Essays on body motion communication.* Philadelphia: University of Pennsylvania Press.
Burke, K. (1969). *A rhetoric of motives.* Berkeley: University of California Press.
Byers, P. (1976). "Biological rhythms as information channels in interpersonal communication behavior." In P. Bateson & P. Klopfer (Eds.), *Perspectives in ethology II.* New York: Plenum Press.
Erickson, F. (1982). "Money tree, lasagna bush, salt and pepper: Social construction of topical cohesion in a conversation among Italian-Americans." In D. Tannen (Ed.), *Analyzing discourse: Text and talk.* Washington, DC: Georgetown University Press.

---

[12] This is a restatement of Pittenger et al.'s "principle of the relativity of signal to noise" (1960, p. 239–240). As they put it , "one man's noise is the same man's signal." In general, their nine "working" principles of human communication are all central and have been forgotten at our loss.

Erickson, F., & Shultz, J. (1982). *The counselor as gatekeeper*. New York: Academic Press.

Garfinkel, H. (1963). A conception of, and experiments with, "trust" as a condition of stable concerted actions. In O.J. Harvey (Ed.), *Motivation and social interaction*. New York: Ronald Press.

Garfinkel, H. (1967). *Studies in ethnomethodology*. Englewood Cliffs, NJ: Prentice-Hall.

Geertz, C. (1973). *The interpretation of cultures*. New York: Basic Books.

Goodwin, C. (1981). *Conversational organization: Interaction between speakers and hearers*. New York: Academic Press.

Grice, H.P. (1975). "Logic and conversation." In P. Cole & J. Morgan (Eds.), *Syntax and Meaning*. New York: Academic Press.

Grice, H.P. (1978). "Further notes on logic and conversation." In P. Cole (Ed.), *Syntax and Semantics*. New York: Academic Press.

Hill, C., & Varenne, H. (1981). "Family language and education: The sociolinguistic model of restricted and elaborated codes." *Social Science Information, 20*, 187–228.

Labov, W. (1972). *Sociolinguistic patterns*. Philadelphia: University of Pennsylvania Press.

Labov, W., & Fanshel, D. (1977). *Therapeutic discourse*. New York: Academic Press.

Labov, W. (1982). Competing value systems in the inner-city schools. In P. Gilmore & A. Glatthorn (Eds.), *Children in and out of school*. Washington, DC: Center for Applied Linguistics.

Lévi-Strauss, C. (1962) [1952]. "Social Structure." In S. Tax (Ed.), *Anthropology Today*. Chicago: University of Chicago Press.

Lévi-Strauss, C. (1953). "Problems of process; results." In S. Tax (Ed.), *Appraisal of anthropology today*. Chicago: University of Chicago Press.

McDermott, R.P. (1977). "Social relations as contexts for learning in school. *Harvard Educational Review. 47*, 198–213.

McDermott, R.P., & Gospodinoff, K. (1979). Social contexts of ethnic borders and school failure. In A. Wolfgang (Ed.), *Nonverbal behavior*. New York: Academic Press.

McQuown, N., Bateson, G., Brosin, H., & Hockett, C. (1971). *The natural history of an interview*. Microfilm Collection of Manuscripts in Cultural Anthropology. Chicago: University of Chicago Library.

Mauss, M. (1967) [1923-4]. *The Gift*. Tr. by I. Cunnison. New York: Norton and Co.

Mead, G.H. (1934). *Mind, self and society*. Chicago: University of Chicago Press.

Mehan, H. (1979). *Learning lessons*. Cambridge, MA: Harvard University Press.

Merleau-Ponty, M. (1973) [1969]. *The prose of the world*. Tr. by J. O'Neill. Evanston, IL: Northwestern University Press.

Pittenger, R., Hockett, C., & Danehy, J. (1960). *The first five minutes*. Ithaca, NY: Paul Martineau.

Radcliffe-Brown, A.R. (1965) [1940]. *Structure and function in primitive society*. New York: Free Press.

Scheflen, A. (1973). *Communicational structure*. Bloomington, IN: Indiana University Press.

Silverstein, M. (1981). "The limits of awareness." In *Sociolinguistic Working Paper, #84*. Austin, TX: Southwest Educational Development Laboratory.

Varenne, H., Hamid-Buglione, V., McDermott, R.P., & Morison, A. (1982). *'I teach him everything he learns in school': The acquisition of literacy for learning in working class families*. New York: Teachers College, Columbia University, Elbenwood Center for the Study of the Family as Educator.

Varenne, H., & McDermott, R.P. (1986). "Why Sheila can read: Structure and indeterminacy in the reproduction of familial literacy. In B. Schieffelin & P. Gilmore (Eds.), *The acquisition of literacy: Ethnographic perspectives*. Norwood, NJ: Ablex.

Chapter 9

On the Necessity of Collusion in Conversation

R.P. McDermott
Teachers College, Columbia University
Henry Tylbor
New York, New York

INTRODUCTION

Language. . . lies on the borderline between oneself and the other. The word in
language is half someone else's. (M.M. Bakhtin, 1934–35)

In 1928, V.N. Volosinov[1] complained that "all linguistic categories, per se,
are applicable only on the inside territory of an utterance" and are of no
value "for defining a whole linguistic entity" (1973, p. 110). This paper
begins with a whole linguistic entity by going beyond the utterance to the
social scene in which it is embedded for a unit of analysis. Unlike some recent linguistic analyses that acknowledge that speech acts do not in themselves provide for discourse cohesion but nonetheless are restricted to
speech acts for a primary focus of investigation, we start with the properties
of social activities as the essential guide to analysis.

We start with some assumptions that are, by now, well informed: participation in any social scene, especially a conversation, requires some minimal
consensus on what is getting done in the scene; from the least significant
(strangers passing) to the culturally most well formulated scenes (a wedding
or a lecture), such a consensus represents an achievement, a cumulative product of the instructions people in the scene make available to each other;

Reprinted with permission from TEXT, 1983, 3.277-297. The present version replaces a
final section on formality with some remarks on power in discourse. Other changes are minor.
This paper was prepared in anticipation of the late Erving Goffman liking it.
[1] Under the guidance and likely authorship of M.M. Bakhtin (Holquist, 1981).

and, because no consensus ever unfolds simply by predetermined means, because social scenes are always precarious, always dependent on ongoing instructions, the achievement of a consensus requires collusion.

Collusion literally means a playing together (from the Latin *col-ludere*). Less literally, collusion refers to how members of any social order must constantly help each other to posit a particular state of affairs, even when such a state would be in no way at hand without everyone so proceeding. Participation in social scenes requires that members play into each other's hands, pushing and pulling each other toward a strong sense of what is probable or possible, for a sense of what can be hoped for and/or obscured. In such a world, the meaning of talk is rarely contained in the "inside territory of an utterance"; proposition and reference pale before the task of alignment, before the task of sequencing the conversation's participants into a widely spun social structure. The necessity of collusion in conversation has wide-ranging implications not only for how people use their talk in conversation, but for how linguistics might profitably locate units for an analysis of conversation.

In this paper, we build a case for the importance of collusion in the organization of talk ("The Case for Collusion") and offer a brief example of how collusion operates in a conversation ("An Example: From Precarious to Treacherous"). From a transcript taken from a videotaped seven-person reading lesson in grade school, we try to give a sense for the complex contexting work people do to arrange for utterance interpretations consistent with, and not disruptive of, the situation the people are holding together for each other. With an example in hand, we attempt to highlight the dimensions of a collusional stand on conversation by contrasting it to the now dominant propositional approach and the recently popular illocutionary approach to language behavior ("Three Ways of Appreciating Language"). Each is discussed in terms of its definition of such fundamental notions as units of analysis, their function, the role of context in their organization, and the theoretical prize won by their description. The relation between collusion and power is addressed in a final note.

THE CASE FOR COLLUSION

Discourses on humility give occasion for pride to the boastful, and for humility to the humble. Those on skepticism give occasion for believers to affirm. Few speak humbly of humility, chastely of chastity, few of skepticism doubtingly. We are but falsehood, duplicity and contradtion, using even to outselves concealment and guile. (Blaise Pascal, 1670)

We build on two common observations on language behavior to develop the claim that collusion is necessary for any conversation. The first observation has it that everyday language is irremediably indefinite, that every utterance indexes or builds on a wide range of knowledge about the world that would require a potentially endless expansion for precise application. The second observation, seemingly contrary to the first, has it that talk is so amazingly exact that participants can often talk their way to long-term concerted activities and well-shared ideas about what they are doing together (often far beyond any agreements immediately obvious in a transcript of their talk).

During the past decade both observations have been secured with much data. Under the banner of pragmatics, we have been shown how much a person must know about the world to understand even brief utterances, and, urged on by sociologists interested in conversational analysis, we have been shown an amazing variety of interactional mechanisms that conversationalists have available for directing and specifying utterance interpretations.

The collusion claim takes both observations seriously. It starts with an appreciation of how much unspecified, and likely unspecifiable, knowledge people must have in order to understand each other. At the same time, the collusion claim recognizes the powers of conversationalists to use local circumstances to shape their knowledge into mutually perceptible and reflexively consequential chunks. This marriage of indefiniteness and precision in utterance interpretation both requires and is made possible by conversationalists entering a state of collusion as to the nature of the world they are talking about, acting on, and helping to create. With a little help from each other, by defining what can (or must) be left vague or made precise, they can shape their talk to fit the contours of the world in which they are embedded, a world they can prolong to make possible further interpretations of their talk.[2]

At its cleanest, conversational collusion is well tuned to people's finest hopes about what the world can be—this often despite the facts, despite a world that sometimes offers them little reason for harboring such hopes. Examples include "we really love each other" or "We can all be smart." Although making believe that such statements are true does not insure our being loved or looking smart, it is an essential first step.

---

[2] Garfinkel (1963) has advanced the same point with his work on "trust" as a condition of stable concerted activities. Various other terms glossing the same phenomenon with varying degrees of consistency and success are "context," "frame," "key," and "working consensus." The term "collusion" adds to these, as Garfinkel would appreciate, a sense of institutionalization and even treachery that we believe essential (institutionalization as the arrangement of persons and commodities that have us necessarily trusting reciprocally in the ways we do; treachery as a measure of how far we will drive ourselves and others to believe in a world not well connected to our experiences).

"Collusion" has the further advantage of plurality, as is essential to any analysis of social behavior such as conversation. One cannot collude alone; it takes at least three persons (as if two to collude and one to interpret).

At its dirtiest, people's collusion amounts to a well-orchestrated lie that offers a world conversationalists do not have to produce but can pretend to live by, a world everyone knows to be, at the same time, unrealizable, but momentarily useful as stated. Examples of collusion as treachery can be cut from the same utterance cloth we used to illustrate collusion as hope. "We really love each other" can still be said when both know the statement as a cover for a relationship that offers only protection from the imagined world beyond the relationship; we have it from marriage counselors that under such conditions demonstrations of love can further lock the participants off from the world and further limit the possibility of their loving each other. Similarly, "We can all be smart" has as its most frequent occasion of utterance the classroom, the very place, as we shall see, in which people organize significant moments during which smartness, and its opposite, must be alternately displayed, recognized, hidden, and held back, in which displays of smartness and stupidity must be choreographed into the relations people have with each other. Without resources for organizing conditions for making possible an experience of love or intelligence, their invocation points more to oppression than to hope.

By lies, we refer to a phenomenon far more prevalent than those in which speakers must first remind themselves what not to say on a future occasion, in which "one has to remember the truth as well as the lie in order to bring consistency to a recriminatory future" that could disprove the lie (Lang, 1980, p. 535). We think this kind of conscious lying is rare relative to the amount of treachery in the world at large. One way of understanding social structure, in fact, is that it offers differential protection from confrontations in which pure lies must be told.[3] Institutional authorities are afforded various shelters from unpredicted accountability. It is possible to live lies

---

[3] As Harvey Sacks (1975) has noted, there are numerous statements across varying occasions to which the "contrast set true-false" is not sequentially relevant. A description of the distribution of occasions for which the contrast set is relevant (and of the various statements that invite its application) might give us a revealing key to social structure. The important point is that talk seems well designed for making delicacy, avoidance, mitigation, and duplicity generally possible. Against this background, it appears that inviting a lie, lying, and catching a liar are socially structured games in which people together ignore the obfuscating powers of language to construct scapegoats and degradation ceremonies. The "outraged jeremiad is the mark of a moralistic rather than a moral society" (Shklar, 1979, p. 24). In this view, conversational "delicacy," for example, an attempt to insure that "the fact that an answerer is not giving [some requested information does] not constitute a recognizable refusal to give it" (Jefferson, 1978), represents a first attempt to escape the onslaughts of a true-false contrast set; lying is a next step for people in situations with fewer social resources for doing delicacy. An appreciation of this fact can help move us from a cynicism about individual morality to a political involvement for making different kinds of morality possible; at best, the outraged jeremiad "is not without affect, because this type of antihypocrite does at least have a sense of what is wrong, rather than an urge to spread the blame" (Shklar, 1979, p. 24).

without having to tell them. Our institutions secure such lives for us at every turn. Starting with the generalized gender configurations available in a culture to specific institutions built around informational entanglements (Hanunoo or Mehinaku courtship, Kpelle secret societies, Mediterranean honor codes, or a therapeutic halfway house for drug offenders in America, and so on), we can find people choreographing each other's behavior according to scores that remain ad hoc and tacit and which, if made explicit, would render the behavior that seems to service them useless. We should never allow ourselves to forget the warning of Nietzsche: "To be truthful means using the customary metaphors—in moral terms: the obligation to lie according to a fixed convention, to lie herd-like in a style obligatory for all..." (1873, p. 47).

The collusion stand on conversation not only unites apparently disparate facts about language behavior (indefiniteness and precision), but holds out the promise of a linguistics that could be useful to an understanding of the social situations in which people do their talking. Although it is a century since George Simmel told us that secrecy is at the heart of any social order and William James told us that hope is a human possibility only by spitting in the face of the odds, our social sciences have proceeded pretty much as if the conditions organizing our lives were well ordered, shared, available for common understanding, and easy to talk about.[4] The social sciences have proceeded oblivious to the basic conditions of our lives together. In the language sciences, this has translated into a focus on the sentence as if truth value or illocutionary force could be found in the utterance.

Now it appears that to account for even the simplest conversations, we have to take seriously the moment-to-moment hopes and lies that connect our utterances into coherent parts of the social order. Language analysis can lead us back to social structure. To the extent that collusion is essential to conversation, then its exploration cannot leave too far behind an account of the institutional constraints that have us colluding in the ways that we do. It will leave us in the long run wondering about the constraints we are work-

---

[4] The alternatives to the natural attitude have been important (Bernstein, 1976). Robert Murphy has offered us a helpful guide in what he calls the first principle of Irish (at least in the sense of not British) social anthropology: "My theories do fit with the well-known Irish trait by which there is little correspondence, and indeed much contradtion, between what a person thinks, what he says, and what he does. Perhaps I can best explain the tenets of Irish Social Anthropology by reversing Durkheim's formulation of the relation between restless, shifting sensate activity and the collective world of norms. My own resolution of the problem, then, is: All things real are ephemeral; all things enduring are false" (1975, p. 55). Edward Casey has directed a similar insight to our understanding of a descriptive enterprise as linguistics must be: "The surface at stake in description is a moving surface. It changes in and through time; and even if such changes are not detectable in a given time interval, their description is itself a temporal event" (1981, p. 199).

ing against that, if we are making up so much of our lives together, we manage often such impoverished versions of what is possible.[5]

Our discussion of the necessity of collusion in conversation could proceed from first principles: All action, said John Dewey, "is an invasion of the future, of the unknown. Conflict and uncertainty are ultimate truths" (1922, p. 12). This is no less true for speaking and listening actors than it is of acrobats and subway riders (whatever the differential in risky outcome). Without a tentative agreement about what the future is (no matter, for the moment, how fanciful or harmful it might be), how else could conversationalists achieve precise understandings from ambiguous materials without ever really saying what is going on? Clearly, conversationalists have to be working together, tripping over the same defenses, stumbling into the same understandings, and working to the same ends (if only to reach the silence at the conversation's end). How they do this work should represent an answer as to how their collusion is both made necessary and subsequently organized.

AN EXAMPLE: FROM PRECARIOUS TO TREACHEROUS

> All lies are collusional; all truths are collusional. The nature of the truth is always bound by the shape of the context. . . . Truth and falsity are matters of agreement. . . . The conditions of sending the signal which arranges for deception may rest in a variety of places within the deception system. (Ray L. Birdwhistell, in McDermott, 1980)

For an example of collusion in conversation, we can offer some talk between a teacher and her first-grade students filmed and analyzed in some detail by McDermott (1976). It is a reading lesson, and much of the interaction is around the issue of getting turns to read. Unlike turns to talk in most conversational clusters, turns to read are not managed just in the pursuit of other conversational goals, but are often the focus of the group. It is in terms of turns to read that the group's talk is made directional, that it takes on meaning and carries social facts. The details of the taking turns to read

---

[5] Grand theories of the world usually include an account of what has to be lied about. Timpanaro has offered a lovely account of a Marx-Freud contrast on the nature of the world that organizes collusion: "It is intriguing to imagine Freud's reaction if one of his patients—a neurotic, but a politically lucid one—in reply to the question which according to Freud was the best means of 'ensnaring' the patient: "What would you consider was the most unlikely thing in the world in that situation? What do you think was the furthest thing in the world from your mind at the time?—had answered: 'I consider the most unlikely thing in the world would be to see a capitalist renounce his own privileges without any use of force on the part of the workers he exploits.' At this point, there would surely have been an exchange of roles: Freud would himself have succumbed to the behavior typical of a 'patient,' he would have lost his temper or changed the subject—in short, have revealed 'resistances' so strong that he would not even have been aware of their existence" (1976, p. 59).

system are constantly put up for noticing, analyzing, and interpreting, and their organization helps to curb the indefiniteness of talk, to make clear, for example, that "Me" is a call for a turn to read or that "Not me" is a request not to read while constituting simultaneously a display of an agreement to listen to another child reading. Collusion is visible in the ways the members have of instructing each other in the use of turns in organizing their interaction and is essential to their production of group order.

The case for the necessity of collusion in conversation is perhaps most arresting in the talk of one child, Rosa, who is often treated as if she had said something different than a literal interpretation of her words would indicate. That is to say, her words, imprecise on their own, are made precise by those about her in ways not well predicted by their propositional content. Literalness aside, how her words are used by the group seems much better described by the conversationalists' situation together as a particular kind of reading group within a particular kind of classroom, school, and wider educational community.

Rosa constantly calls for a turn to read by shouting "I could" or "I could read it." In addition, she complains when she is bypassed, "G. . Go around" or (long later and still without a turn) "I wanna go around." But Rosa almost never gets a turn to read; she is understood to be not very good at reading, and her status as a turn-taking reader seems to be problematic enough to be commented on at various times during the children's half-hour at the reading table with the teacher. Upon careful examination, it seems that Rosa is doing much work to arrange *not getting a turn:* everyone is on page 5, Rosa on page 7 (as everyone can tell with a first grade illustrated reader); as the teacher begins to call on another child, Rosa calls for a turn, just a fraction of a second behind; as the other children move up from their books to face their teacher and to call for a new turn, Rosa lowers her head into the book with her face turning away from the teacher. The ploys are numerous in kind and fast in occurrence.

Linguists have not had enough trouble with the kind of duplicitous talk just described. It has been unfortunately easy to put aside. Propositional analysis can chalk it up to the abominations of actual use in social scenes. However great the evidence to the contrary, no matter how much conversationalists seem to rely on meaning one thing by saying another, traditional linguistic analysis remains intact by claiming that the *literal* meaning of an utterance must remain the point of departure for describing how speakers understand each other.[6] The argument is that the meaning of Rosa's calls

---

[6] Owen Barfield (1947) has pointed out that the best of our talk, metaphor and poetry, thrives on saying one thing to mean another, the more one meaning lives as a modification of another, the richer the metaphor. Linguists have managed to avoid a careful look at how such talk is used in social life by giving great sway to the grammatical and referential workings of language. Nietzsche has bemoaned how deep this trend runs: "I am afraid we are not rid of God because we still have faith in grammar" (1889, p. 34).

for a turn to read are quite clear; how else could have they been transformed
into something systematically different from a literal reading. In addition,
such a transformation in use would have been most likely signaled linguis-
tically by some marked appeal to irony or subterfuge. However transformed
by the situation, for most linguists, propositions remain meaningful in their
own terms.

Illocutionary analysts would take Rosa a little more seriously. They
would try to extrapolate the actual conditions of the social actors that their
intentions could protrude without anyone having very literally put them
into words. Again, the propositions would be understood on their own,
albeit in a series. In either case, Rosa would be understood cognitively, as a
strategist, who was manipulating the social scene and the people in it with
her words. What would have organized her words or their systematic interpretation would have been left undiscovered. Neither Rosa nor linguistics
would have been well served.

The collusional approach to Rosa's talk forces us to take her situation
much more seriously. We are not interested simply in speakers, or even
speaker-hearer pairs and the ways they react to each other. Rather we are interested in ongoing social scenes into which people walk and talk their lives
together. As Arthur Bentley said well long ago:

> Terminology has been poor in the social sciences, drawn as it has been from
> the language of everyday life—from the vocabularies of the manipulation of
> one man by another. But not the point of view of one toward another is what
> we seek, rather the very processing itself of the ones-with-others. (1926, p. 457)

We are not interested in Rosa the strategist, but Rosa the participant. Rosa's
words, Bakhtin reminds us, are only half her's. They must be brought to completion by the group. And all their words together, if well enough studied,
belong to the conversation which is in turn a moment in a far more extensive
conversation we might call American education (Varenne, 1983).

A collusional approach takes it that Rosa does not act on her own; that
the very machinery used to transform, reframe, or to put into a new key
Rosa's talk is group-produced; that every member of the group helps to in-
struct Rosa to say what she says in favor of what she did not say, which, in
fact, if she did say would break the conditions for the group being together in
an order that they can recognize, use, and perpetuate.

The collusional stand further takes it that the work members do to construct a consensus (that we are all learning how to read) while allowing, ignoring, and hiding important exceptions (namely, that some of us are here
only to not get caught not knowing how to read) is a direct product of the
institutional conditions under which the teacher and children are asked to
come to school. Their production and interpretation of talk must be understood as a product of their collusion in response to a complex institutional

setting that requires that they talk as if they could all learn while they arrange much of their day catching each other not learning (Hood, McDermott, & Cole, 1980). In taking up utterances that seem to mean the opposite of what they would on their own appear to say, we have moved from collusion as a necessary solution to the precariousness of everyday life situations to collusion as a defensive tactic against the treachery of everyday life. There are reasons for "using even to ourselves concealment and guile." When further pressed, there are reasons for lying even to others, although we must remember, before hunting down liars, that "the conditions of sending the signal which arranges for deception may rest in a variety of places within the deception system."

It is not easy to describe an instance of collusion in conversation. One effort, particularly directed to linguists, is available in a recent paper by Dore and McDermott (1982). The dedicated reader can examine that data analysis in the light of the more radical arguments of the present account. The argument of that paper is that a particular "I could read it" by Rosa, by virtue of how it is said and its timing, is seemingly accepted as such by everyone in the group while they simultaneously act as if she had said that she could not read it and that a particular someone else had been given the turn to read. Rosa's claim for a turn appears at a time when the group is somewhat at bay for a clear defintion as to what they are doing together. By interpreting Rosa's utterance as something different from what it seemingly proposed, an interpretation Rosa helped them to, the members of the group used Rosa's call for a turn to establish both a turn and a reader (other than Rosa) for the turn. The point is that everyone used the primary practice of the scene, namely, the constant evaluation of every reader's skill and the avoidance of such evaluation by different members at various times, to understand Rosa's call for a turn as a suggestion that she be bypassed. The very conditions that allowed for the methods Rosa used to instigate her subterfuge were not only well recognized by the group, they were maintained and supported by every member's involvement with evaluation.

The present paper offers a different fragment of talk from Rosa's reading group (Table 1). The scene opens with the teacher calling on Child 4 (numbered in order around the table). Child 1 and Child 2 have read page 4 to the group. Rosa is Child 3. As the teacher and the children raise their heads as Child 2 finishes page 4, the teacher turns her head towards Rosa, who has moved her head further down into the book and right, away from the teacher's advancing gaze. The teacher continues turning her head left, past Rosa, until she reaches Child 4. She calls on him, "Alright. Let's see you do it." He moans a complaint, "Unnh." Rosa begins to suggest that they take turns in order: "G. .Go around". She is supported almost immediately by Child 4 screaming, "What about Rosa. .Sh. .She don't get a turn." Child 5 begins to chide Rosa, "You don't get a. . .", while Child 2 also calls for a more rigorous linear order, "Yeh. Let's go around." The

TABLE 1.   Transcript of Procedural Positioning, Getting a Turn 3

Teacher:	Alright. Let's see you do it.
Child 4:	Unnh
Rosa:	G...go around
Child 4:	What about Rosa (screaming) Sh..she don't get a turn.
Child 5:	(to Rosa) You don't get a...
Child 2:	Yeh. Lets go around.
Teacher:	Jimmy (very softly). You seem very unhappy. Perhaps you should go back to your seat.
Rosa:	Back to Fred, then back to me. No. Back to Fred, back to Anna, and back to Fred and Maria and back to me.
Teacher:	Alright, Fred. Can you read page 4?

teacher then, after a nonvocalized false start and a nervous glance away, addresses Child 4 very softly, "Jimmy. You seem very unhappy. Perhaps you should go back to your seat." Simultaneous with the teacher's attribution of Jimmy's feelings, Rosa begins to lay out the order of the going around that she has called for; in none of the two or three versions she suggests is there any discernable, going-around order. After Rosa has her say, the teacher calls on Child 6, "Alright, Fred. Can you read page 4?"

How can we understand Rosa's talk? Is she calling for a turn, seeming to call for a turn, simply showing that she knows some rules about turn-taking in rounds, or, as we suspect, arranging to not read while nonetheless appearing to be part of the group? The point of this paper is that there is no one answer to this question. Rosa's "G...Go around" may contribute all the readings just listed. Some are more interesting than others in supplying insight to life in classrooms, and some are used more than others at various subsequent moments by group members. We should not expect Rosa to have a uniform stand serviced by her words. In the complex role that teaching-learning scenes play in the lives of young children, could we expect Rosa to be free of all the tensions of her community around the issues of relative skill, smartness, competitiveness, and the like?

As we flee from utterance complexity to a consideration of social context for some key to what Rosa might be talking about, we are offered some relief by the fact that Rosa's utterance does not stand alone. The question of meaning must be rephrased: What instructions are available in the scene for the participants to organize an interpretation of Rosa's utterance? Part of the instructions, of course, is Rosa's utterance; her talk reflexively arranges its own context and helps to organize the conditions for its own interpretation. And what does Rosa's utterance have to work with in arranging a hearing?

First of all, the group is organized posturally into a procedural focus or positioning well suited for activities such as getting a turn to read (for criteria establishing postural-kinetic events and their importance to the structure of interaction, see McDermott, Gospodinoff, & Aron, 1978; Scheflen, 1973). That they are at a getting-a-turn-to-read relevant moment is everywhere available in their body alignments and attentional structure. Second, that such moments are delicate can be seen in the work members do to preserve them; for example, they all attend carefully to the beginning and ending of every positioning and hold each other accountable for any disruptions of the apparent order. Third, within any positioning, alternative formulations of what might be going on between the participants are often attempted and usually abandoned; for example, while most are still calling for a turn-to-read, someone might start reading. Fourth, while working hard keeping a focus organized and rejecting rival formulations, members of the group constantly make available for use the dimensions along which they can understand each other; for example, a child who does not follow the pattern of a procedural positioning may be considered a management problem, whereas a child who does not follow a pattern in a pedagogical positioning may be understood as a learning problem. Fifth, there appears to be a strong preference for how and when different dimensions can be applied; for example, the smart-dumb continuum is constantly applied in classrooms, and much interactional delicacy must be organized to apply the continuum only in cases when someone can be called smart. The application of the continuum to instances of "dumb" behavior does occur, but participants usually work hard to have it not noticed. Sixth, a getting-a-turn positioning does not usually attract the application of a smart-dumb contrast set, and it is accordingly used as a moment safe from intelligence evaluations. By virtue of its comparative safety, it is used often as a place in which the participants prepare for some next intelligence display, including preparation for who might be subject to an upcoming evaluation. It is therefore a perfect umbrella under which to perform covert, unspoken evaluations that organize for more public contests in the next moment.

With all this going on (and the reader, for purposes of this paper, has only to agree that such events could be at work; it would take a volume to complete a description of the behavioral background), Rosa's utterance enters the world pregnant. As Bakhtin noted well: "Language is not a neutral medium that passes freely and easily into the private property of the speaker's intentions; it is populated—overpopulated—with the intentions of others. Expropriating it, forcing it to submit to one's own intentions and accounts, is a difficult and complicated process" (1934–35, p. 294).

The utterance is shaped to fit its occasion. The conditions that organize its production and interpretation are distributed throughout the system.

To the extent that "G...Go around" represents a hope, the possibility (no matter how improbable at the moment) of Rosa learning to read well enough to perform must be organized by all the participants. To the extent that it represents an institutionalized lie, a delicate way to avoid a confrontation with a smart-dumb contrast set, that too has to be organized across persons. Indeed, the lie has to be told against the background that everyone is still hoping, or at least making believe that they are hoping, that Rosa can learn to read.

Instead of asking whether Rosa is intending to get a turn—an unanswerable question anyway—if we asked about the social constraints to which Rosa's remark might be an appropriate and constitutive reaction, then we have to ask how the participants are playing into each other's hands (that is, more literally, colluding) to organize the world Rosa gets systematically instructed to avoid. If we could ask more questions about what issues our every institution has us avoiding, we would have not only a better account of social structure, but a better account of the language tools people use to build social structure.

THREE WAYS OF APPRECIATING LANGUAGE

The salient aspect of the social fact is meaning; the central manifestation of meaning is pragmatic and meta-pragmatic speech; and the most obvious feature of pragmatic speech is reference. We are now beginning to see the error in trying to investigate the salient by projection from the obvious. (Michael Silverstein, 1981)

There are a number of dimensions along which to rank different approaches to language behavior. Silverstein (1979) goes to particular pains to point out what cannot be accomplished with traditional analyses that focus on reference and what might be accomplished if we were to concentrate more immediately on the social facts produced with talk. This paper proceeds in that spirit. By starting with the collusion required of conversationalists, the social facts of which the people are a part move to the center of analysis and their language can be understood for what it does within the social order. This approach gives us a different way of appreciating language behavior. It also requires a shift in some of the tools we have used to do language analysis.

In the following chart (Table 2), we offer a simple scheme for contrasting a collusional approach to appreciating what people do with their talk with the more traditional propositional and illocutionary approaches that dominate contemporary linguistics. At its best, the chart should offer a snapshot of what each of the approaches is trying to accomplish and its underlying conceptual assumptions.

The propositional approach focuses on the sentence for a unit of analysis, understands sentences in terms of their referential potential, and asks questions about their clarity and possible truth value. Propositional analyses produce statements of the type, Sentence X can mean *a, b,* or *c.* The variation in meanings available in the sentence is understood as contained

TABLE 2. Three Ways of Appreciating Language

	Units of Analysis	Function of Talk	Role of Context	Analytical Accomplishment
Propositional Analysis	Scenes and social facts	Reference	An occasionally necessary afterthought to cover possible transformations under supposed conditions of actual use.	Utterance X means a or under special well-marked circumstances b or c
Illocutionary Analysis	Speaker-hearer propositions and intentions.	Expression and manipulation	A frequently necessary afterthought to explain how apparent social conditions regularly alter canonical propositional meanings to express speaker intentions.	Utterance X means a under conditions a, b under conditions b, c under conditions c, where the conditions are defined by phenomena beyond the talk, such as statuses and roles, that transform the talk.
Collusional Analysis	Scenes and social facts	Alignment and linkage, institutional maintenance and social change	An essential dimension of language analysis. As behavior reflexively organizes its own contexts, talk can be appreciated for how it organizes its own interpretation as a sequentially relevant element in a social scene.	Utterance X helps to preserve and organize the conditions for its own interpretation as a constitutive element of social scene. Institutional treachery and social transformation are constant possibilities around which interpretation are reflexively organized.

within the sentence. Context is irrelevant and invoked only in the face of the abominations of actual use; it has no systematic bearing on utterance interpretation. Meaning is framed by the capital and the period without any reference to how, as Frake (1980) reminds us, plying frames can be dangerous or in any other way consequential for speakers.

An important, if partial, advance is made in the linguistic sciences when analysts start to look at the consequences of talk, at the effects speakers have one upon another. For a unit of analysis, speech act theorists stick closely to the sentence although they focus on what the sentence is doing in conjunction with other sentences. The utterance exchange is the purported unit of analysis, although the descriptions are deemed complete with the attribution of intentions. Talk is understood as being about the expression of intentions, and variations in utterance interpretation are chalked up to the complexities of organizing an identity in social situations; thus, hedging and mitigating can rule the discourse. The analytic product gives an appearance of being more complete than propositional analyses.

Dimensions of context are considered crucial to the description of the illocutionary force of speech acts. However, the use of context in the analysis is nonetheless an afterthought. There is still a reliance on a soup-in-the-bowl approach to context. According to this model, the soup has a life of its own; it is the substance which is placed in a bowl and accordingly shaped. In speech act analysis, propositional meaning is the soup (an alphabet soup, most likely, good for monologue, reference, and description) and the social statuses and roles of the speaker-hearer pairs are the contexts that organize the rewrite rules allowing the referential power of talk to be obscured enough to meet the demands of the social situation. Reference remains primary in the analysis, and the conditions of context are plied against what anyone could recognize as the canonical interpretation.

The problem with the soup-in-the-bowl approach is that it allows the assumption that the soup exists independent of the bowl, that the meaning of an utterance remains, if only for a moment, independent of conditions that organize its production and interpretation, that meaning exists "on the inside territory of an utterance." If, however, soup and bowl, behavior and its contexts, utterance and the hierarchy of scenes it serves, are all mutually constituted, then the utterance cannot stand alone; it cannot make meaning on its own any more than a fiber can make a rope, or a thread a fabric.[7] An

---

[7] Bateson is essential here: "It is important to see the particular utterance or action as part of the ecological subsystem called context and not as the product or effect of what remains of the context after the piece which we want to explain has been cut out from it" (1972, p. 338). Birdwhistell adds an equal wisdom in an account of what a context is: "I like to think of it as a rope. The fibers that make up the rope are discontinuous; when you twist them together, you don't make *them* continuous, you make the *thread* continuous... The thread has no fibers in it, but, if you break up the thread, you can find the fibers again. So that, even though it may look in a thread as though each of those particles are going all through it, that isn't the case. That's essentially the descriptive model" (in McDermott, 1980, pp. 4, 14).

utterance can only help to piece meanings together, and in so doing erases itself as the essential unit of analysis. Along with many other behavior sequences, an utterance becomes consequential in social fact, and it is to these facts we must turn for instructions on how to appreciate language as a social tool.

The collusion approach develops from a more reticular sense of context. It rejects the traditional notion of intention-to-mean as directly homing in on its object, but instead recognizes that the pathway of meaning with talk is by no means simple and assured. The behavioral stuff to which an utterance can make connections, and the connections the utterances make possible, are primary in the analysis. The irremediable absence of strict borders between persons and others, between acts and other acts, produces interactional puzzles that require constant alignment and collusion from participants (Plessner, 1965; Wieder, 1974). As we saw in some moments in Rosa's life, talk is primarily about alignments with others—alignments that run a moral order gamut from institutional manipulation to social transformation for the good of all, talk that runs the moral order gamut from hiding and lying to a will to believe and consciousness-raising. An appreciation of talk as collusional raises the most basic human issues for our consideration. It is demeaning to the richness of talk and its talkers to limit its description to anything less than a consideration of the most fundamental issues facing people in social life.

REMARKS ON COLLUSION AND POWER

The necessity of collusion in conversation raises two issues for the analysis of power in discourse. The first issue concerns how an analyst can find power in talk. Linguists have not solved this problem, nor indeed have they tried very hard. The solution will not be easy. The interactional residue apparent in even the most obvious patterns of form use, for example, the use of address terms or honorifics (French "tu" and "vous" and Japanese 'keigo" forms being classic), has produced little insight into the more complex constraints operative in a social structure. The more subtle interactional dynamics underlying differences in timing, for example, in the frequency of interruptions and strategic silences (as between men and women), although important for orienting us to power issues, have not been any more helpful in supplying us with an exact calculus for locating the dynamics of power in social relations.

By its emphasis on plurality, a notion of collusion suggests that we give up the question of *who* has particular powers and move instead to questions of how social institutions offer *access* to various kinds of power and how various conversational sequences supply instructions to their participants for acting consequentially for the institution of which they are a moment.

We do not need to know who is powerful; rather, we need to identify the resources supposedly powerful people have available and the instructions within the power system that keep them, by simply following their nose, knowing how to wield their powers. By focusing on the collusion between the apparently powerful and the apparently impotent, conversational analysis may alert us to the institutional constraints on communicative activities.

By its emphasis on institutional treachery, a notion of collusion goes further to raise the question of what people have to arrange *not to talk* about in order to keep their conversation properly con-sequential with the institutional pressures that invade their lives from one moment to the next. Bateson once noted that the key question to be asked of any situation is what one would have to do to tell the truth while a participant (in Birdwhistell, 1977). This is a crucial remark, for a description of the constraints on people telling the truth, indeed of their even conceiving what a telling of the truth might be, represents a good description of the powers made available, fought over, or shied away from in a conversation (which is but a moment in the life of a more inclusive set of constraints called an institution). Institutional analysis might proceed by addressing conversational data with questions about what can be talked about while at the same time being kept quiet, handled delicately, lied about in a pinch, or confronted only under the most dire circumstances.

The second issue concerns what linguistics would look like if it were to take seriously that matters of institutional access and power are at the heart of most conversations. Gone would be a preoccupation with propositions that carry their own self-contained meaning, between sentence capital and period. The lonely speaker would give way to a community of voices, the proposition to the social fact. Gone also would be the speaker-hearer pair totally circumscribed within their own competencies, jockeying intentions back and forth in the name of felicity (although often behind her back). Speakers and hearers would instead merge into a language collective, struggling to wrestle meanings to the ground and to sequence them into the harsh realities of institutional constraints.

This paper addresses both issues by way of an example of collusion in conversation taken from some classroom talk that is impossible to understand, at least as the participants understand it, without reference to the social structural constraints in terms of which some things not easy to say nonetheless seem to dominate the conversation. That it is an American school, first grade reading lesson conversation, as significantly different, for example, from an American family conversation, a Hanunoo or Balinese reading lesson conversation, or even an American school lunch conversation, makes a great difference in the understandings available to the participants in their interpretation and use of their own talk. In American schools, children must learn that the borders between competence and incompetence are not clearly defined, but subject to constant social rearrangement. Class-room discourse is dominated by questions of "Who can?" and, just as importantly, but far less often stated, "Who cannot?" This fact about classroom life is ubiquitous in transcripts from classrooms and the key to their interpretation (the same key the participants can be shown to be using in their orientation to both the said and the unsaid).

REFERENCES

Bakhtin, M.M. (1981). Discourse in the novel. In M. Holquist (Ed.), *The dialogic imagination*. Austin: University of Texas Press. (Original work published 1934-35)
Barfield, O. (1962). Poetic diction and legal fiction. In M. Black (Ed.), *The importance of language*. Englewood Cliffs, NJ: Prentice-Hall. (Original work published 1947)
Bateson, G. (1972). *Steps to an ecology of mind*. New York: Ballantine.
Bentley, A. (1926). Remarks on method in the study of society. *American Journal of Sociology, 32*, 456-460.
Bernstein, R. (1976). *The reconstruction of social and political theory*. Philadelphia: University of Pennsylvania Press.
Birdwhistell, R.L. (1977). Some discussions of ethnography, theory and method. In J. Brockman (Ed.), *About Bateson*. New York: Dutton.
Casey, E. (1981). Phenomenological method and literary description. *Yale French Studies, 61*, 176-201.
Dewey, J. (1922). *Human nature and conduct*. New York: Random House.
Dore, J., & McDermott, R.P. (1982). Linguistic indeterminacy and social context in utterance interpretation. *Language, 58*, 374-398.
Frake, C.O. (1980). *Language and cultural description*. Stanford, CA: Stanford University Press.
Garfinkel, H. (1963). A conception of, and experiments with, 'trust' as a condition of stable concerted activities. In O.J. Harvey (Ed.), *Motivation*. New York: Roland Press.
Holquist, M. (1981). The politics of representation. In S.J. Greenblatt (Ed.), *Allegory and representation*. Baltimore: Johns Hopkins University Press.
Hood, L., McDermott, R.P., & Cole, M. (1980). Let's try to make it a good day. *Discourse Processes, 3*, 155-168.
James, W. (1967). *The writings of William James* (J. McDermott, Ed.). New York: Random House.
Jefferson, G. (1978). What's in a 'nyem'? *Sociology, 12*, 135-139.
Lang, B. (1980). Faces. *Yale Review, 71*(4), 533-540.
McDermott, R.P. (1976). *Kids make sense: An ethnographic account of success and failure in one first grade classroom*. Doctoral dissertation, Anthropology, Stanford University (Ann Arbor: University Microfilms, 1977).
McDermott, R.P. (1980). Profile: Ray L. Birdwhistell. *The Kinesis Report, 2*(3), 1-4; 14-16.
McDermott, R.P., Gospodinoff, K., & Aron, J. (1978). Criteria for an ethnographically adequate description of concerted activities and their contexts. *Semiotica, 24*, 245-275.
Murphy, R.F. (1975). The quest for cultural reality: Adventures in Irish social anthropology. *Michigan Discussions in Anthropology, 1*, 48-64.
Nietzsche, F. (1954). 1873. On truth and lies in an extra-moral sense. In F. Kaufmann (Ed.), *The portable Nietzsche*. New York: Viking Press. (Original work published 1873)
Nietzsche, F. (1968). *Twilight of the idols*. London: Penguin. (Original work published 1889)

Pascal, B. (1966). *Pensees*. London: Penguin. (Original work published 1670)

Plessner, H. (1965). *Die Stufen des Organischen und der Mensch*. Berlin: de Gruyter.

Sacks, H. (1975). Everyone has to lie. In M. Sanches & B. Blount (Eds.), *Sociocultural dimensions of language use*. New York: Academic Press.

Scheflen, A.E. (1973). *Communicational structure*. Bloomington: Indiana University Press.

Shklar, J. (1979). Let's not be hypocritical. *Daedalus, 108*, 1–25.

Silverstein, M. (1979). Language structure and linguistic ideology. In R. Clyne, W. Hanks, & C. Hofbauer (Eds.), *The elements: A parasession on linguistic units and levels*. Chicago: Chicago Linguistic Society.

Silverstein, M. (1981). The limits of awareness. *Working Papers on Sociolinguistics*, no. 84. Austin, TX: Southwest Educational Development Laboratory.

Simmel, G. (1964). *On individuality and social forms* (D. Levine, Ed.). Chicago: University of Chicago Press.

Timpanaro, S. (1976). *The Freudian slip*. New York: NLB.

Varenne, H. (1983). *American school language*. New York: Irvington.

Volosinov, V.N. (1973). *Marxism and the philosophy of language*. New York: Academic Press.

Wieder, D.L. (1974). *Language and social reality*. The Hague: Mouton.

Author Index

Subject Index